Other Books by Frederic Fairchild Sherman

Landscape and Figure Painters of America

American Painters of Yesterday and Today

Albert Pinkham Ryder

John Ramage: A Sketch of His Life and a List of His Portrait Miniatures

Early American Portraiture

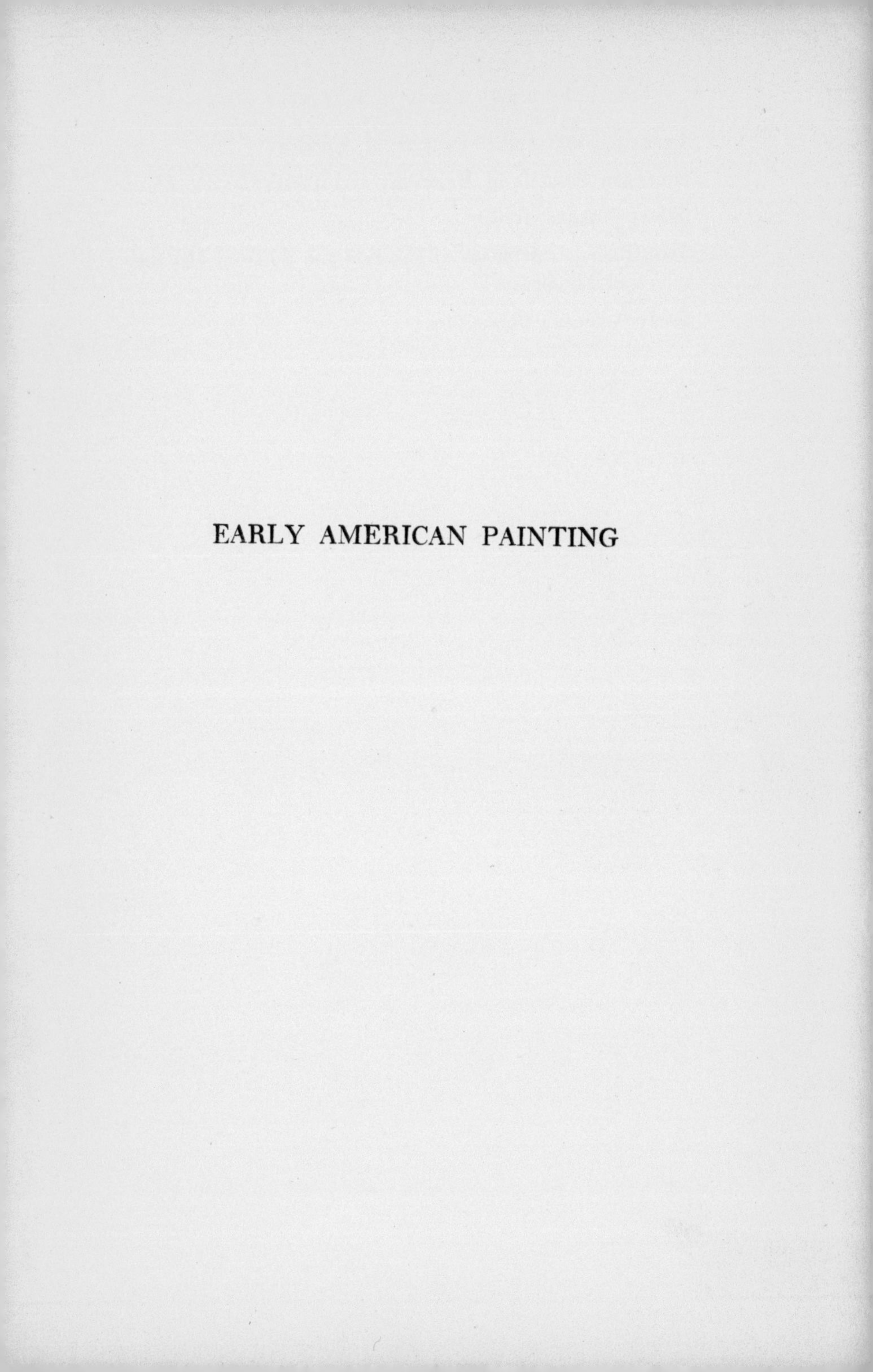

EARLY AMERICAN PAINTING

Century Library of American Antiques

WALDO R. BROWNE, *General Editor*

EARLY AMERICAN POTTERY AND CHINA
John Spargo

EARLY AMERICAN FURNITURE
Charles Over Cornelius

EARLY AMERICAN GLASS
Rhea Mansfield Knittle

EARLY AMERICAN COSTUME
Edward Warwick and Henry C. Pitz

EARLY AMERICAN PRINTS
Carl W. Drepperd

EARLY AMERICAN SILVER
C. Louise Avery

EARLY AMERICAN TEXTILES
Frances Little

EARLY AMERICAN PAINTING
Frederic Fairchild Sherman

IN PREPARATION

EARLY AMERICAN BOOKS AND PRINTING
John T. Winterich

Lee-Phillips Portrait

GEORGE WASHINGTON

By Gilbert Stuart

Early American Painting

By Frederic Fairchild Sherman

Illustrated

The Century Co.

New York *London*

17

First Printing

PRINTED IN U. S. A.

TO THE MEMORY OF

HENRY WALTERS

Whose friendship and encouragement
were a source of inspiration for over
twenty years

PREFACE

BEFORE the middle of the seventeenth century there were in what is now the United States few residences or even public buildings large enough for the exhibition of paintings, and that reason alone, had there been no other, would have discouraged any attempt at art. It is interesting to note that painting, at least in the field of portraiture, began to be practised in the American Colonies as soon as place was found for the display of pictures. In Virginia, the colonization of which was begun in 1607 by the English, the advent of the artist was considerably delayed. In New York, which the Dutch, who began to settle there about 1614, named New Netherland, Jacobus Gerritsen Strycker produced a portrait of his brother Jan in 1655. In the colony of Massachusetts Bay, settled by the English in 1628, William Reed made a portrait of Governor Richard Bellingham in 1641; and in what is to-day South Carolina, whose first permanent settlement was made by the English in 1670, Henrietta Johnston, an Englishwoman, painted a likeness of Robert Johnson in 1718. John Smibert, a Scotchman who came to Newport, Rhode Island, in 1728, finished in 1729 his large group representing Bishop Berkeley and his family; Pieter Vanderlyn executed a likeness of Johannes Van Vechten in 1719; and John Watson, a Scotchman who had settled in New Jersey in 1715, produced a portrait of Sir Peter Warren in 1731. Peter Pelham, who came to Boston in 1726, probably painted the next year his likenesses of the Rev. Cotton Mather the eminent New England divine, who died in 1728. Henri Couturier, a Dutchman who settled in New Amsterdam early in the seventeenth century, made a portrait of Frederick Philipse in 1674—after the region was conquered by England.

Thus we see that the earliest painting in America was exclusively in the field of portraiture. The first artists, without exception, were foreign limners who found meager opportunities for the exercise of their talents in making likenesses of the landed gentry and Colonial officials of their day—or, failing that, as in the case of Strycker, painted portraits of themselves and members of their immediate families. As a natural consequence, the influence of the art of

Holland and England especially is predominant in early painting in this country. Strycker's portraits, which are unquestionably the best of these works, are in the Dutch tradition, reminiscent of Rembrandt and his school; Couturier's are in the slightly artificial manner of French portraiture of the time; and the likenesses of Peter Pelham and Smibert exhibit the stiffness and formality that characterized the work of contemporary English artists—qualities that continued to dominate the creation of our painters until the vital touch of Gilbert Stuart impregnated American portraiture with life. His influence is almost immediately apparent in the work of his contemporaries.

It was not until well into the eighteenth century that anything like a native school of portraiture began to emerge—and then only, of course, in the work of a few painters such as Matthew Pratt and John Singleton Copley. Pratt's first instructor was his uncle, James Claypoole, and his first portrait probably that of Benjamin Franklin, painted in 1756. Copley's first master was his father-in-law, Peter Pelham, and his first likeness supposedly that of William Welsted of Boston, now lost—of which, however, Copley made an engraving. Welsted died in 1753, when the artist was fifteen. Innumerable American artists of the eighteenth century were entirely self-taught, many of them beginning as sign- or coach-painters, some even as house-painters; and probably most of them, at least at first, prepared their own colors, made their brushes, stretched their canvases, and planed their panels. Not a few began modestly as craftsmen, engravers, or draftsmen, rather than as painters, and it is remarkable that so great a number managed finally to attain distinction as artists of ability.

Many of the early American-born painters studied at one time or another with Benjamin West in London. It is to West's credit that their works are in no sense imitative but exhibit definite personal characteristics, a fact which in no wise detracts from West's influence as a teacher in their development as artists. The reality of this influence in the formation of their style, many of our early painters individually acknowledged. In the ensuing pages the reader will encounter numerous references to the historical compositions which they painted in West's studio; but almost invariably their subsequent productions were in other fields of artistic expression, the great majority of them having become portrait-painters. John Trumbull and Washington Allston, whose religious and historical subjects constitute a considerable portion of their contribution to American art, were notable exceptions.

In Colonial and Revolutionary times the portrait-painter customarily lived in the families of his sitters, and his board constituted a substantial part of the remuneration for his labors, the remainder probably consisting of negotiable commodities in the main, with a small monetary payment. In the pursuit of his profession he traveled a good deal, from one place to another—often, it is reasonable to infer, afoot, notwithstanding which, he appears to have been highly respected and to have enjoyed the favor of the well-to-do, who alone could afford to employ him.

The first American painters of miniatures are of the eighteenth century. It was not until social life had developed on a scale of relative importance that these elegant objects of art, in their lockets of gold, found favor with the élite; then, however, their popularity never vacillated until the introduction of the daguerreotype, which marks the beginning of their decline in favor and in artistic excellence. During the brief period in which miniature-painting flourished here as an art, our country produced two of the greatest of all miniaturists, Edward Greene Malbone and Charles Fraser, both of whom were native-born and their work almost exclusively American.

It is pertinent to add here that many of the so-called American "primitives," in the way of portraits, are anything else than what they are termed, most of them being in reality the pot-boilers of inferior painters of the early nineteenth century who, unable to find employment in the cities, scoured the country districts, painting atrocious portraits for whatever they could get for them. Some of these daubers started out with a wagon-load of canvases on which the bodies of men and women and the backgrounds were already painted, and only the heads to be added. Thus they were able to do a good business with little effort if their work—or, more likely, their prices—recommended them to the residents of any particular locality; and certain localities are to this day overrun with their pictures.

Preface

Numerous dealers in antiques, and some art dealers as well, offer them for sale from time to time as "primitives." Primitives they certainly are not—as already made clear. Furthermore, they are worthless as works of art or of antiquity.

In the following pages, the chief practitioners in portrait- and miniature-painting are treated chronologically. Each section devoted to an individual artist provides, when possible, information as to where representative works of the artist may be seen in public galleries. Preceding each division is given a chronological list of the artists dealt with in that division, with the dates of birth and death (one or both) when these could be ascertained—otherwise a date at which the artist is known to have been working. The year 1850 marks the end of the period covered in the main text.

Except in a very few instances, no foreign painter who worked in this country but did not settle here permanently is mentioned. On the other hand, all American-born artists, even those—notably, Benjamin West—who lived permanently abroad, are scrupulously retained.

While the object of the volume is not to offer a

critical estimate of the work of all or any of the artists whose names appear in its pages, criticism is not avoided. The author's intention is to present a survey of the whole field of early painting in this country, and to give as much as is necessary in the way of fact to enable the reader to form his own opinions about the relative importance of the various painters.

I wish to express my thanks to the owners of the many pictures reproduced, for their courtesy, and to Mr. Frederick W. Coburn, Mr. William McKillop, Mr. George Dudley Seymour, and the Ehrich Galleries for assistance given me in assembling material which has been of real service. The bibliography at the end of the volume indicates the various sources of information upon which I have drawn.

CONTENTS

ILLUSTRATIONS

Illustrations

Illustrations

PART I

PORTRAIT-PAINTERS OF THE SEVENTEENTH CENTURY

LIST OF PAINTERS

William Reed	English	1607–1679
Henri Couturier	French?	—— 1684
Jacobus Gerritsen Strycker	Dutch	—— 1687
Evert Duyckinck	Dutch	1621–1702
Thomas Child	English?	—— 1706
Jeremiah Dummer	American	1643?1718
Henrietta Johnston	English	—— 1728
Gerret Duyckinck	American	1660?1710
Evert Duyckinck 3d.	American	1677–1727
N. Byfield	American	1677 ——
Gustavus Hesselius	Swedish	1682–1755
Peter Pelham	English	1684–1751
John Watson	English	1685–1768
Pieter Vanderlyn	Dutch	1687–1778
John Smibert	Scotch	1688–1751
Gerardus Duyckinck	American	1695–1742

PART I

PORTRAIT-PAINTERS OF THE SEVENTEENTH CENTURY

PORTRAITURE in America in the early days is rather generally characterized by certain very definite limitations. These limitations have to do chiefly with a lack of invention in the matter of pose, resulting in monotony; and with a stereotyped technic. The painter's technic is his real source of power. Our early portrait-painters, with few exceptions, worked in a dry, commonplace technic that defeated their highest purpose. They managed, however, within the limitations of a too marked definition of line and a too obvious insistence upon the minutiæ of inessential detail, to produce acceptable and even commendable likenesses. A very few of our artists of a later date, like Gilbert Stuart, whose technic was the creation of his brush, managed to make portraits that were not merely likenesses but works of art. The freedom of Stuart's manner of painting and the elegance of his style are obvious. They enabled him to develop a technic comparable to that of the greatest portrait-painters, and to paint portraits that rank with those of the recognized masters.

William Reed

The first settlement in that part of America which is comprised in the United States was made in Virginia in 1607, by the English, reinforced in 1610 by Lord De La Warr. Though the English landed at Plymouth, in what is now the State of Massachusetts, in 1620, the colony of Massachusetts Bay, where the first American portrait was painted by William Reed, an English artist, in 1641, was not settled until 1628.

This canvas represents the governor of the colony, Richard Bellingham (1592–1672), and is inscribed "Govr. R. Bellingham. Effigies Delin. Boston. Anno. Dom. 1641 Ætatis 49. W. R." Boston, where it was painted, was at the time the chief settlement in the English colonies in America. Even so, it was a very modest village, the population as late as 1700 not exceeding seven thousand. The first State House, or government headquarters, was not built until 1659, eighteen years after Reed had painted this likeness.

The artist emigrated from Batcomb, England, in 1635, and settled originally in Weymouth. Here he resided until 1646, when he moved to Boston. Nineteen years later, in 1665, he was commissioned to draw the earliest map of the Massachusetts Bay Colony, from which fact one may conclude that he enjoyed a considerable reputation as an artist. Probably he was well acquainted with Governor Bellingham, whose portrait he painted, for six years after it was finished we find him elected Deputy of the General Court.

It is entirely reasonable to assume that Reed was the only painter established in this country at the time. The portrait of Bellingham is, however, sufficient evidence that the artist had studied to some advantage as a youth in England. His command of his medium and the quality of his draftsmanship give proof of unquestioning confidence on his part, and the canvas is not at all the primitive sort of production that would indicate an untrained talent.

For the identification of the painter we are indebted to the late Thomas B. Clarke, who by process of elimination among the various "W. R.'s" in the colony of Massachusetts Bay at the time Governor Bellingham's portrait was painted, found but one, this William Reed, whose abilities included any graphic talent whatsoever.

Jacobus Gerritsen Strycker

The second American portrait was painted by Jacobus Gerritsen Strycker in 1654, in the Dutch town of New Amsterdam, now the city of New York. The artist was a man of means and decided culture; a farmer, a trader, and a magistrate, who practised art, presumably, more as a pastime than as a profession—a supposition supported by the fact that two of his three known works represent his brother and himself. He painted Adrian Van der Donck (1618–55) in 1654, his own brother Jan (1617–97) in 1655, and at about the same time the self-portrait—all of them in the Dutch manner, on wooden panels.

Strycker, who came to America in 1651, was born in Ruinen, in what is now the province of Drenthe in the Netherlands. That he must have studied to advantage under one or another of the Dutch masters of the seventeenth century before he emigrated to

Thomas B. Clarke Collection

PLATE I

GOVERNOR RICHARD BELLINGHAM

Painted in 1641 by William Reed

this country, the quality of his product leaves no doubt whatever. He was by far the most proficient of our early painters, and the only one who may be said to have something definite in the way of an individual style and a suggestion of genius.

This artist occupied a position of importance in the life of his time, and had a successful public career. He was a burgher in 1653, and later an alderman of New Amsterdam and attorney-general and sheriff of the Dutch towns on Long Island. He died in 1687. It is interesting to conjecture what the development of portraiture in our country would have been if the Dutch had succeeded in holding their possessions here, and the artistic influence of Strycker, reinforced by that of later arrivals trained in the Dutch school, had molded it upon the style of the great Dutch masters.

Henri Couturier

While the records upon which is based the identification of Henri Couturier, the third American painter, prove him to have been of Dutch origin, his surname and given name, as well as the character of his portraiture, go far toward convincing us that he was at least of French descent and probably studied art in France. He came to America about 1660 and settled in New Amsterdam, where in 1674 he painted Frederick Philipse (1626–1702), of Philipse Manor in Yonkers. The portrait shows him to have been a trained artist, and exhibits the elegance of style and slightly artificial arrangement characteristic of the French school. Technically it is a conspicuously noteworthy performance for its time, in this country, and indicates a more careful training than that of most of our early painters.

Couturier's identity was proved by discovery of his monogram—the same with which his canvases are signed—on the register of a list of goods sent to him from Holland in 1663 by his son Jacob, who had adopted the Dutch form of his name, spelling it "Coetrier."

Evert Duyckinck

Evert Duyckinck, the first of the most important family of painters in Colonial America, was born in Holland in 1621, and came to New Amsterdam in 1638. He is variously described in records of the time as a limner, a painter, a glazier, and a burner of

Thomas B. Clarke Collection

PLATE II

FREDERICK PHILIPSE

Painted in 1764 by Henri Couturier

glass. In 1685 he painted a likeness of William Stoughton (1631–1701), who in 1692 was appointed Lieutenant-Governor of the Province of Massachusetts; and in 1693 one of Stephanus Van Cortlandt (1643–1700), a work of indifferent quality though of considerable historic interest. Van Cortlandt became the first American-born mayor of New York City, in 1677, and in 1697 was made first Lord of the Manor of Cortlandt.

Duyckinck's sons Gerret and Evert 3d, and his grandson Gerardus, also were professional portrait-painters. Examples of the work of all four of these artists may be seen at the New York Historical Society, and others unquestionably might be found among the possessions of old Dutch families surviving along the Hudson River. Save in exceptional instances, these works are of little or no artistic value, whatever their historic interest as documents of their time.

Gerret Duyckinck, Evert Duyckinck 3d and Gerardus Duyckinck

Gerret Duyckinck, son of Evert, born in New Amsterdam in 1660, was the second American-born painter. In all probability his father was his first and only instructor. His product reinforces this conclusion, inasmuch as the resemblances between the work of the father and that of the son are perfectly obvious. It is a type of portraiture quite uninspired, and almost its only interest for us to-day is the fact that it preserves for posterity the features of persons eminent in the colonies in their day.

Evert 3d, another son, and the grandson Gerardus both worked in the same stilted manner. The former painted Ann Sinclair Crommelin, his first cousin, in 1725, and the latter, James de Lancey (1703–60), who was Chief Justice of New York under Governor Clinton, and acting governor of the province from 1753 to 1755.

Jeremiah Dummer

Curiously enough, William Dunlap, in his "History of the Arts of Design in the United States"—for many years the recognized source-book in its field—makes no mention of Jeremiah Dummer, the earliest American-born artist.

Dummer was a noted gold and silver smith, as well as a portrait-painter, during the last quarter of the seventeenth century, in Boston, and must have been a person of some importance in the community. Born in Newbury, Massachusetts, in 1643 or 1645, he was the son of Richard Dummer, an official of the Massachusetts Bay Colony from 1635 to 1636. His self-portrait, inscribed "Jeremiah Dummer pinx. Delin. Anno. 1691. Mei Effigies. Aetat 46," is still in the possession of direct descendants in Wilmington, Massachusetts. His likenesses are comparable to the better ones of those by other artists of his day in this country; and considering his priority as an American-born painter, one is at a loss to account for the almost complete neglect he has suffered from students and historians of American art.

Henrietta Johnston

The first Southern painter, Henrietta Johnston, was also the first woman artist in America. She practised portraiture, mainly in pastel or crayons, as early as the first quarter of the eighteenth century in what is now South Carolina. It is more than likely that she had already painted some likenesses before 1700, however, for she died in 1728, and unless she came to America at or about the former date she would certainly have begun the practice of her art before that year. In 1725 she painted three pictures in New York for Colonel Moore which are among the finest of her works in pastel. Her earliest known portrait is that of Sir Nathaniel Johnson, dated 1705. The only work in oil from her hand with which I am acquainted is the portrait of Robert Johnston (1677–1735), last Proprietary Governor of the Carolinas, dated 1718.

Henrietta Johnston's work, especially in pastel, has a distinct charm and makes a decided appeal. Virtually all of her portraits are privately owned and not often accessible to the public, though examples appear from time to time in various loan exhibitions.

N. Byfield

N. Byfield, probably Nathaniel Byfield, Jr., the son of Nathaniel and Deborah Byfield, was born in Boston on November 14, 1677. A signed and dated portrait from his brush, said to represent Richard Middlecott (who died in 1704), painted in 1713, was shown at the loan exhibition of "One Hundred Colo-

Thomas B. Clarke Collection

PLATE III

JAN STRYCKER

Painted in 1655 by Jacobus Gerritsen Strycker

nial Portraits" at the Boston Museum of Fine Arts during the summer of 1930. The patent superiority of his style to that which prevailed in New England in his day is the measure of its merit in a sense. Simple and dignified in arrangement, broadly painted, and with skilful rendering of expression in the face, it makes one eager for the discovery of further likenesses from this artist's brush.

Thomas Child

Another Colonial artist, only one of whose canvases we have, is Thomas Child, who died in 1706. His portrait of Sir William Phipps (1651–95), Sheriff of New England in 1688 and Governor of the Province of Massachusetts from 1692 to 1694, must have been painted in the last quarter of the seventeenth century. It was shown in the 1930 exhibition at the Boston Museum of Fine Arts.

This canvas, like Byfield's, in excellence is above the average of its time, broadly and freely painted, and altogether pleasing in its unaffected air of actuality.

Gustavus Hesselius

Many of the earliest portraits in the old families of Maryland were painted by Gustavus Hesselius, a Swedish painter who came to these shores in 1711, landing at Christinaham, now Wilmington, Delaware, and going to Philadelphia. He married and settled eventually in Annapolis, where he was probably the first instructor of Charles Willson Peale in oil painting.

Rembrandt Peale called Hesselius a portrait-painter of the school of Kneller. His self-portrait and that of his wife may be seen at the Historical Society in Philadelphia; and in the permanent collection of the Cleveland, Ohio, Museum of Art are his portraits of Judge William Smith and his wife, signed and dated "G H 1729."

Hesselius' son John studied with him and later painted portraits, almost entirely in Philadelphia and the South.

Peter Pelham

The English artist, Peter Pelham, born in 1684, came to Boston with his family in 1726, and in 1784

Boston Athenæum, Boston, Massachusetts

PLATE IV

LIEUTENANT-GOVERNOR WILLIAM STOUGHTON

Painted in 1685 by Evert Duyckiuck I

married the widow of Richard Copley, whose son, John Singleton Copley, then eleven years of age, was to become the greatest of our early portrait-painters. Pelham's likenesses of Cotton Mather, the eminent New England divine—or one of them, at least—must have been painted before 1728, in which year Mather died. Pelham also painted the contemporary portraitist John Smibert (1688–1752), as well as John Cushing (1695–1778), who was Justice of the Massachusetts Supreme Court from 1747 to 1771.

This artist probably was the first instructor of his stepson, John Copley, and his own son, Henry Pelham, who became one of the best of our native Colonial miniaturists. Pelham's portraits of the Rev. Cotton Mather are exhibited at the American Antiquarian Society in Worcester, Massachusetts.

John Watson

John Watson, born in 1685, an Englishman who came to the American Colonies in 1715, set up his easel the same year in the Colonial capital of New Jersey, Perth Amboy. In 1741 he painted that distinguished naval officer Sir Peter Warren (1703–

52), who was presented with the freedom of the city of New York and married the same year Susan de Lancey, the daughter of Stephen de Lancey. Sir Peter was a member of the Council of New York, under Governor Clinton, from 1743 to the time of his death in 1752. His house, built in 1740, was situated on the property now bounded by Bleecker, Fourth, Charles, and Perry streets, in what is to-day the center of the Borough of Manhattan, or New York City proper.

Watson was a rather prolific painter, but as most of his portraits are unsigned, many of them are as yet unidentified. He is reputed to have worked a good deal in Delaware and as far south as Maryland, and to have painted miniatures as well as oils. A number of pencil portraits from his hand have been discovered.

Pieter Vanderlyn

A Dutch artist, Pieter Vanderlyn, painted innumerable portraits for the early Dutch families of New York. They are palpably uninspired though perhaps acceptable likenesses, and are not to be compared with the earlier works of his fellow-

Thomas B. Clarke Collection

PLATE V

JOHANNES VAN VECHTEN

Painted in 1719 by Pieter Vanderlyn

countryman Strycker, which are infinitely superior in every sense. Vanderlyn's portrait of Johannes Van Vechten (1676–1742), painted in 1719, one of his best canvases, was formerly in the Clarke collection, exhibited for several years at the Philadelphia Museum. John Vanderlyn, a very proficient portraitist of a later date, was a grandson of this artist.

John Smibert

One of the last of the seventeenth-century portrait-painters who worked in the American Colonies, the Scottish artist John Smibert, was the most prolific of them all, and a great many admirable specimens of his work remain to acquaint us with his abilities, which were not inconsiderable.

Born in Edinburgh in 1688, Smibert came to this country with Bishop Berkeley, arriving at Newport, Rhode Island, in 1729, and later settled in Boston, where he soon became popular as a painter of the Colonial aristocracy. Many of the best likenesses we have of the leading magistrates and preachers of New England and New York who lived between 1729 and the year of Smibert's death, 1751, are from his brush.

Smibert had brought with him to this country numerous copies he had made of the Old Masters in Europe, and these later probably influenced materially such artists as Copley and Allston in the formation of their style.

Smibert's earliest American work is the large group of 1729, representing Bishop Berkeley and his family, the sketches for which he may have made on the voyage across the Atlantic. This great canvas may now be viewed at the Yale Art Gallery in New Haven, Connecticut. His likenesses of Stephen de Lancey (1663–1741)—who built the house which after his death became Fraunces Tavern in New York City—Governor Joseph Wanton of Rhode Island, and the three grandsons of Captain Peter Oliver, prove him to have been a really capable portraitist.

PART II

PORTRAIT-PAINTERS OF THE EIGHTEENTH CENTURY

Collection of Mr. Luke Vincent Lockwood, New York City

PLATE VI

FRANCES MOORE

Painted in 1725 by Henrietta Johnston

LIST OF PAINTERS

Thomas Hudson	English(?)		1701–1779
Nathaniel Emmons	American		1704–1740
Robert Feke	American		1705–1750
Joseph Badger	American		1708–1765
Jeremiah Theus	Swiss		1719–1774
Charles Bridges	English	Working	1730–1750
Abraham Delanoy	American	Working	1730–1750
James Claypoole	American		1720–1796
John Greenwood	American		1727–1792
John Hesselius	American		1728–1778
John Woolaston	English	Working	1750–1767
Joseph Blackburn	Scotch (?)	Working in the	1750's
Robert Edge Pine	English		1730–1788
Nathaniel Smibert	American		1734–1756
Matthew Pratt	American		1734–1805
John Singleton Copley	American		1738–1815
Benjamin West	American		1738–1820
Charles Willson Peale	American		1741–1827
Henry Benbridge	American		1744–1812
Samuel King	American		1749–1819
James Peale	American		1749–1831
John Durand	American(?)	Working	1767–1782
Ralph Earl	American		1751–1801

Adolph Ulrich Wertmuller	Swedish	1751–1811
John Johnston	American	1752–1818
Gilbert Stuart	American	1755–1828
Joseph Wright	American	1756–1793
John Trumbull	American	1756–1843
Samuel Broadbent	American	1759–1828
James Sharples	English	1761–1811
Edward Savage	American	1761–1817
Mather Brown	American	1761–1831
Robert Fulton	American	1765–1815
William Dunlap	American	1766–1839
Ezra Ames	American	1768–1836
Richard Jennys	English	Working 1798
Henry Sargent	American	1770–1845
John Rubens Smith	English	Working 1812–1849
John Vanderlyn	American	1775–1852
Jacob Eichholtz	American	1776–1842
Rembrandt Peale	American	1778–1860
Washington Allston	American	1779–1843
John Wesley Jarvis	English	1780–1839
Samuel L. Waldo	American	1783–1861
Thomas Sully	English	1783–1872
John Paradise	American	1783–1834
John J. Audubon	French	1785–1851
James Frothingham	American	1786–1864

Matthew Harris Jouett	American	1787–1827
Samuel F. B. Morse ..	American	1791–1872
Chester Harding	American	1792–1866
James Barton Longacre	American	1794–1869
William Jewett	American	1795–1874
Lucius Munson	American	1796–1822
John Neagle	American	1796–1865
Nathaniel Jocelyn ...	American	1796–1881
Asher B. Durand	American	1796–1886

American Antiquarian Society, Worcester, Massachusetts

PLATE VII

THE REV. COTTON MATHER

Painted before 1728 by Peter Pelham

PART II

PORTRAIT-PAINTERS OF THE EIGHTEENTH CENTURY

THE eighteenth century may be said to have witnessed the inauguration of the American school of portraiture. Though native-born artists of an earlier day were influential in contributing to the nucleus of knowledge upon which such painters as Matthew Pratt, John Singleton Copley, Gilbert Stuart, and James Frothingham formed a distinctive style of pictorial representation, it was only after 1750, and in the works of these painters and a few others, that a style different from that of previous days and foreign contemporaries, and approximating a recognizable type characteristic of this country, is apparent. While its product represented nothing notably individual, it nevertheless exhibited certain variations that sufficiently distinguish it as a distinct school emerging from the inherited mannerisms of foreign masters, whose works constituted the bulk of our portraiture to that time.

This native school was already in its decline before the death of Gilbert Stuart, and the middle of the nineteenth century saw its final disintegration. The best of the portrait-painters born in the early eighteen hundreds—such men as Henry Inman, James Reed Lambdin, and Charles Loring Elliott—were but imitators of the style of an earlier day. Stuart, the greatest of our portrait-painters, was not a product of the American school; nor was his work, in the main, the specifically American type of portrait, though such a picture as the "Mrs. Richard Yates" is sufficient to show how powerfully the native influence in art moved him at times. Indeed, typically American portraiture never found a master capable of realizing its possibilities. All we have to indicate its character are a few isolated likenesses of surprising quality; for example, those by Matthew Pratt, Copley's "Mrs. Fort," Stuart's "Mrs. Yates," and some of Frothingham's works. The influence of English portraiture smothered the natural and national tendencies of our painters.

The characteristics of this native portraiture were an emphasis of the individuality of the sitter, achieved by picturing a person in a natural attitude rather than in a prescribed "pose," and a facility seldom surpassed—indeed, rarely equaled—of imparting to a face more than a little of the mobility of life, which in a sense gives a painted likeness the look of a living presence.

Thomas Hudson

Of Thomas Hudson, our earliest-born portrait-painter of the eighteenth century, I am unable to find any biographical information at all. Presumably he was of English descent, and he may not have come to America until about 1750, at which time the two portraits from his hand now recorded seem to have been painted. That of Jonathan Belcher (1681–1757)—a Boston merchant who served as Governor of Massachusetts and New Hampshire from 1730 to 1741 and of New Jersey from 1747 to 1757—is an admirable canvas in the somewhat artificial style of the time. It may be seen at Harvard University, to which it now belongs.

Nathaniel Emmons

A likeness of Jonathan Belcher was painted in 1738—while he was Governor of Massachusetts and New Hampshire—by Nathaniel Emmons, the second American-born artist who worked in Boston, and who occupied the residence which, after his death, became the home of another Colonial painter, John Smibert. Only five likenesses by Emmons have been identified so far; they include those of Andrew Oliver, Governor Belcher's nephew, and Oliver's friend, Samuel Sewall, besides the canvas of 1738 mentioned above.

Robert Feke

Robert Feke, born at Oyster Bay, Long Island, in 1705, is the earliest native-born artist whose portraits, to any considerable number, have been identified and listed, and about him a serious biographical and critical monograph has been published. The painter's self-portrait, owned by the Rev. Henry Wilder Foote, author of the monograph just mentioned, is one of Feke's best canvases, many of which

Thomas B. Clarke Collection

PLATE VIII

SIR PETER WARREN

Painted in 1731 by John Watson

are hardly more than mediocre performances. The large group of 1741 representing "The Royall Family," which may be seen at Harvard University, illustrates to advantage his real abilities. The best of his canvases are rather impressive, but the poorer ones are entirely negligible as works of art. He is known to have practised in Newport, Rhode Island, where he married, and in Boston, New York, and Philadelphia.

Joseph Badger

Seventy or eighty likenesses have been identified as coming from the hand of Joseph Badger, who was born in Charlestown, Massachusetts, in 1708. Such works of his as I am acquainted with, both in half- and full-length, are hardly more than average portraits for their time, and entirely lacking in any individuality that would entitle them to even a modicum of distinction. The "Captain John Larrabee," a full-length, and the likeness of Richard Wibird (1702–65), a half-length, are fair specimens of his portraiture. It is of a type that barely escapes banality.

Jeremiah Theus

The Swiss painter Jeremiah Theus, who went to South Carolina, in 1739, executed portraits there for over thirty years. He was the most popular artist of his day in Charleston, and painted virtually all of the élite, including the Manigaults, Alstons, Haywards, Warings, Ravenels, Izards, and others of social or political prominence.

Some idea of Theus's capabilities may be gathered from the fact that Charles Fraser, one of our greatest miniaturists, owned one of his likenesses, which he said he valued for their excellence. According to another estimate of the early nineteenth century, quoted by Dunlap, "his pictures were as stiff and formal as the originals, when dressed for the purpose and sitting for them . . . though the faces were painted with great care."

The fact that likenesses by Theus, having been neglected for years, are now much sought after, is another indication of their merits, which have led them sometimes to be mistaken for canvases from the easel of John Singleton Copley, to whose work they have never more than a superficial resemblance.

Property of Mr. Paul Mascarene Hamlen

PLATE IX

SELF-PORTRAIT

Painted in 1691 by Jeremiah Dummer

While relatively few portraits from Theus's brush have thus far been identified, this artist probably painted literally hundreds of them in the course of his long residence in Charleston.

Charles Bridges

Charles Bridges, an English artist who painted many portraits in Virginia from 1730 to 1750, was an indifferent imitator of the style of Sir Peter Lely and Sir Godfrey Kneller. Many of his canvases have been erroneously attributed to the latter. His women may be almost invariably recognized by a certain arrangement of a lock or curl of hair, appearing on or in front of a shoulder. The "Evelyn Byrd," illustrated in the Bayley-Goodspeed edition of William Dunlap's book, is one of the more pleasing of his portraits. His inability to paint drapery and costume with any degree of success is apparent in this canvas, though pose, expression, and background are managed with a sufficient amount of skill to redeem the picture as a whole and insure it a place apart from and above the simply literal likenesses produced by lesser painters.

Abraham Delanoy

One of the earliest recorded American students of Benjamin West in London was Abraham Delanoy, a native of New York, who advertised as a portrait-painter in that city in January of 1771. The likeness he painted of Peter Van Brugh Livingston—president of the first provincial congress of New York, called in 1775—a small canvas, about twenty by fifteen inches in size, is the only portrait from his hand which I have seen. It belongs to the Thomas B. Clarke collection and has been exhibited for several years past at the Philadelphia Museum.

James Claypoole

Of the works of James Claypoole of Philadelphia, the teacher of Matthew Pratt, few are known to us to-day. Claypoole was the first American-born artist in Pennsylvania, a man of means and public spirit, and sheriff of Philadelphia from 1777 to 1780. His daughter Maria married James Peale, the miniaturist.

It is said that when Claypoole left Philadelphia

it was with the intention of joining Benjamin West in London. He broke his voyage, however, to visit Jamaica, and died there about 1796. The single likeness from his brush which I have seen, the "Margaret Hamilton Allen" of the Clarke collection, was painted in 1746. From the circumstances of his life I should infer that his essays in portrait-painting were undertaken more as a pastime than as a profession, and that they were few in number.

John Greenwood

At the early age of fifteen, as was customary at the period, John Greenwood the painter was apprenticed to Thomas Johnston, an engraver in Boston. As he left this country in 1752 and did not return, all of his American portraits were painted before that date. The signed likeness of Benjamin Pickman (1708–73) was painted in 1749. It is hardly probable that many of these American works survive, but so far as one may judge from the Pickman portrait, which is at the Essex Institute in Salem, Massachusetts, they are not likely to have been of any particular artistic significance.

John Hesselius

John Hesselius, son of the noted Swedish artist Gustavus Hesselius, was born in Maryland in 1728. As a matter of course he studied painting with his father, and his earliest portraits were painted in Maryland, mostly in the vicinity of Annapolis, his home. For several years he practised his profession successfully in Philadelphia, where he painted likenesses of two members of the Walton family in 1752. After his father's death in 1755 he went to Virginia, and from there returned to Maryland. In 1775, four of his works, representing Colonel Charles Carter and his wife Anne, and Anne Champe and her husband, were bequeathed by the latter, John Champe, to Mrs. Champe. The likeness of Thomas Johnson (1732–1819), first Governor of the State of Maryland, whose son married the artist's daughter, was painted in 1768.

John Woolaston

The American reputation of the English painter John Woolaston is unquestionably founded upon his early and rather intriguing full-length portrait of

Martha Washington. His double portrait of two children of her first marriage, John Parke and Martha Custis, however, is the very quintessence of the commonplace. The little figures are exaggerated in size in proportion to the canvas, and constructed with no more understanding of the semblance of life than one would expect to encounter in a pair of dolls.

Woolaston came to this country about the middle of the eighteenth century, and was working here as late as 1767, practising his art in New York City, Philadelphia, and the South, and painting his most satisfactory canvases in New York between 1751 and 1757. Among his likenesses are those of John Randolph's grandmother, painted in the South, Governor Hardy of New York, William Allen of Claremont, New York, Captain Archibald Kennedy (1718–94), Brigadier-General Lewis Morris (1726–98) of the Continental Army and his wife Mary Walton Morris (1727–94), and John Stevens (1708–92), member of the Continental Congress. The last six are all of his New York period.

Robert Sully wrote William Dunlap in the early years of the nineteenth century that Woolaston's pictures were much in the Kneller style, more feeble than that of Reynolds but with a very pretty effect. That seems a not too extravagant characterization of his portraiture, and may be accepted as fairly accurate.

Joseph Blackburn

Joseph Blackburn, who painted portraits in Boston, Massachusetts, Portsmouth, New Hampshire, and other New England towns in the seventeen-fifties, was probably a Scotch artist, taught in England, who visited this country for but ten or twelve years, and of whose entry and departure there is no record extant. He is included here chiefly because of the influence his portraiture—like that of John Smibert—had upon John Singleton Copley, the first American-born artist to reach eminence in this field.

Blackburn's manner of signing his canvases—almost invariably "I Blackburn"—led to his being known as "Jonathan" Blackburn until the discovery in 1919, in Brooklyn, New York, of a portrait signed "Jos. Blackburn." He is well represented in our public galleries, examples of his work being contained in the permanent collections of the Boston and Worcester museums, in the Metropolitan Museum of Art in New York City, and in the Rhode Island School of Design at Providence. His finest works, however, with the notable exception of the "Commodore Tyng" at the Yale Art Gallery, are all privately owned, including his portraits of Susan Apthorp (1754–1815), Sir Jeffrey Amherst (1717–97), Mrs. James Otis, Jr. (1728–89), and the large "Winslow Family."

Robert Edge Pine

Robert Edge Pine, an English historical painter and "artist to the King," who came to this country in 1784 with the intention of doing a series of pictures portraying the outstanding events of the Revolutionary struggle, remained to add some notable portraits to his credit, which preserve his reputation to posterity. His "Congress Voting Independence," painted in the very room where that event took place, an invaluable historical document and by no means a negligible work of art, is the only canvas of the contemplated series which he ever executed.

Robert Morris, the Revolutionary financier, became Pine's patron, and built for the artist a house in Eighth Street, Philadelphia, besides which Morris undoubtedly assisted him in getting commissions for portraits in that city as well as elsewhere. Pine's likeness of the Hon. Francis Parkinson, a work of considerable distinction, may be seen at the Pennsylvania Historical Society. Many of his portraits were painted in Baltimore and at Annapolis, including in the former city the large family groups of the Pattersons and the Robert Smiths, and the likeness of General Smallwood (1732–92), that distinguished officer in the Continental Army who afterward became Governor of Maryland. The "Carroll Family" was painted at Annapolis and Pine's portrait of General Washington was done at Mount Vernon in 1785.

Nathaniel Smibert

The three known canvases by Nathaniel Smibert, son of John Smibert, who died when but twenty-two, justify the belief that had he lived to maturity he might have outranked as a portraitist John Singleton Copley, who was his contemporary. The large portrait of Ezra Stiles, sometime President of Yale College, in the Yale Art Gallery, the most ambitious of these

Metropolitan Museum of Art, New York City

PLATE X

MISTRESS ANN GALLOWAY

By Gustavus Hesselius

works, is unquestionably the most important, and suffers the least from comparison with similar works from Copley's hand. That of John Lovell (1710–78), principal of the Boston Latin School from 1734 to 1775, which may be seen at Harvard University, is a more interesting and, I think, more artistic creation, besides being perhaps the earliest of the works of the distinctively American school, antedating Matthew Pratt's likenesses of himself and the Wests.

I invite the reader to turn to the reproduction of the portrait by Thomas Child, to see how plainly in it one may note the beginnings of what eventually materialized in the American school of portraiture. In the main, of course, the works of our greatest portrait-painters, such as John Copley, Gilbert Stuart, Mather Brown, and but recently John Sargent, are certainly not in the distinctively native tradition. Their prototypes are to be found in the realm of English portraiture.

Matthew Pratt

The first distinctively American portrait-painter, Matthew Pratt, was the son of a Philadelphia goldsmith who was a personal friend of Benjamin

Franklin. Pratt's earliest known portrait is one of Franklin, now at the Manor House in Yonkers, New York; this was painted in 1756, when the artist was but twenty-two. Betsey Shewall, the fiancée of Benjamin West, was related to the young artist, who accompanied her and West's father to London, and represented the bride's father at her marriage to West.

It was at this time that Pratt painted the likenesses of Benjamin West, Mrs. West, and himself, which first indicate his personal style and distinguish him as the father of the American school of portraiture. Simple in pose, unmarred by extravagances of dress, sober and refined in color, and carried out with an exquisite understanding of inherent possibilities of effective portrayal of individuality, sincerity, I should say, is their significant attribute. His style is notably more personal and national than that of John Singleton Copley, who was but three years his junior and already a well-established portraitist in Boston when Pratt's first canvas was painted. The majority of Copley's likenesses betray their indebtedness to foreign, and particularly English, models; he excelled as a delineator of dress rather than as a

Yale Art Gallery, New Haven, Connecticut

PLATE XI

BISHOP BERKELEY AND FAMILY

Painted in 1729 by John Smibert

portrayer of character as evidenced by feature or expression.

For years after Matthew Pratt became a well-recognized portrait-painter in Philadelphia, he eked out his living by painting signs for tradesmen and others, many of which continued to hang in that city long after his death. John Neagle, himself an artist of no small merit in a later day, said that they were broad in effect and loaded with color . . . that there was no niggling in his style or touch . . . and that in a great measure they stirred a spirit within him for art. Pratt's large group of "The American School," representing himself and other embryo artists in the London studio of Benjamin West, dated 1765, is now at the Metropolitan Museum of Art in New York, and the portraits of West and his wife are at the Pennsylvania Academy of Fine Arts in Philadelphia.

John Singleton Copley

John Singleton Copley, who is so generally thought of as the first of our native school, was in reality of Irish descent though born in this country. Of decided British leanings at heart throughout his life, he left America for the island kingdom in 1774, never to return, and eventually settled in London. As a boy he must have profited by study of the copies of the Old Masters which hung in the elder Smibert's painting room, and gained something at least from familiarity with that artist's likenesses.

His earliest portrait, that of William Welsted, Copley engraved in 1753, when but fifteen. As early as 1765 he was established as a professional portrait-painter in Boston, and by 1771 lived in something of splendor in that city, dressing with ostentatious elegance. In that year he visited Philadelphia and Brunswick, New Jersey, and later New York City, where he painted a total of thirty-seven canvases in a period of seven months.

Upon his arrival in England in 1775, Copley challenged the fame of Benjamin West in the field of historical composition; but quickly recognizing that portraiture, appealing as it does to the vanity and affections of men, offered greater financial reward, he returned to that branch of art, in which he gradually acquired a lasting reputation and by means of which he amassed a generous fortune. As a historical painter he was ineffectual because of the very trivialities that are a decoration to his works in portraiture. He seemingly was naïve enough to think that ermine, feathers, glossy boots, and glittering emblems and buckles were the stuff whereof historic events are made memorable. A sorrier example of misunderstanding in relation to an essential feature in any branch of painting it would be hard to find.

It is but natural that Copley's style should be modeled upon the British type of portraiture. The first likenesses he saw as a lad in Boston were stamped with the inherited characteristics of that school and produced by its expatriate practitioners in the New World city of his birth. The portrait of his half-brother, Henry Pelham, known as "The Boy with the Squirrel," is probably the least British, the most truly American, of his early works. Curiously enough, it was also the first of his canvases exhibited in London, where in 1766 it gained the young artist an unusual celebrity.

Except for this work, the beautiful circular "Self Portrait," and the "Mrs. Seymour Fort" at the Athenæum in Hartford, Connecticut, virtually all of the innumerable remaining likenesses from Copley's hand are almost stereotyped effigies in the English manner, elegant in the painting of costume, resplendent in imitation of the glittering effect of emblems and jewels, affected in pose, and unsatisfactory as to any revealing indication of character or disposition by features or facial expression.

In 1767, when he was twenty-nine, Copley was well known to those interested in art on both sides of the Atlantic, a regular exhibitor in London though still practising his profession successfully in Boston. Benjamin West, who was in great favor at the British court in the early seventeen-seventies, was generous in his recognition of Copley's merit, a fact which Copley was courteous enough and sensible enough to appreciate, though some of the other less gifted and less amiable of his contemporaries who profited by West's encouragement were not.

At the height of his career in this country, Copley received fourteen guineas for half-lengths and was fast becoming financially independent. At any rate, in 1774, when he departed from America, it was with ample funds in hand for a three-year period of travel and study in the Old World, and it is reasonable to infer that he left with his aged mother a considerable sum besides, to insure her comfort in his absence.

Property of the Hon. William Tudor Gardiner, Augusta, Maine

PLATE XII

SIR WILLIAM PHIPPS

By Thomas Child

With the elegance of the type of portraiture he is famous for in one's mind it is incongruous to think of him as "very thin, pale, a little pock-marked, with prominent eyebrows and small eyes," and yet that is the only description we have of his personal appearance to enable us to visualize the man—excepting, of course, the self-portraits, which tell quite a different story and are very likely more than a little idealized. It is easy to conjecture that his manner was just a trifle that of one who was not without conceit, and who was rather inclined, if at all indisposed, to indulge too readily his feelings.

Further than that, the above-quoted testimony of an artist named Carter, his companion in the Italian days, is unconvincing. Judged by what we know of the man from his actions and his art, John Copley was indubitably refined, considerate, appreciative of every kindness, and precise in his acknowledgment of any favor. Upon his tact and his wit it is surely unnecessary to expatiate, inasmuch as without them, with all his skill, he could not have successfully competed in the London of his day with the established leaders of the British school.

His likenesses were no more the peers of those

emanating from the studios of Reynolds, Romney, and Gainsborough than they were the equals of the best of those of his fellow-countrymen, such as Mather Brown and Gilbert Stuart. Even so little known a portraitist as Robert Field, whose art is identified with America, was certainly Copley's equal if not his superior in some of the likenesses he painted in Canada at the beginning of the last century, while Copley was still living.

Copley's technic is impersonal, and fails to vitalize the images he transcribes. Consequently his faces have the fixity of masks or the frozen look of those in Mrs. Jarley's wax-works. Compared with the canvases of really great portrait-painters, his likenesses are seen to rely too obviously upon his dexterity, the ineffectual accuracy of merely competent draftsmanship. They have everything but the semblance of life—the most important thing of all, that which alone makes a portrait great and therefore a great work of art. Those whom Copley painted seem to have been arbitrarily posed to suit the requirements of his extravagant ideas of impressive composition, and with little or no regard for the customary and characteristic attitudes of his sitters, which, it should

Harvard University, Cambridge, Massachusetts

PLATE XIII

GOVERNOR JONATHAN BELCHER

By Thomas Hudson

not be forgotten, are quite as revealing as the human physiognomy. Only the "Mrs. Seymour Fort" is quite natural and convincing in pose, a requisite which Matthew Pratt and Willson Peale, perhaps less skilful as mere painters, achieved easily enough.

Of the manner of Copley's painting, the records all substantiate the point of the argument in this estimate of his art. It was said in his lifetime that "no man ever knew how to manage paint better" than he did, which presumably meant that he had in the highest degree the ability to make it simulate the sheen of silk and satin, the glitter of gilt and jewels, and the like. Furthermore, it was said that his manner "was very mechanical," and "mechanical" describes quite accurately many of his portraits. Charles Robert Leslie, who in his day was somewhat of a critic as well as an artist, wrote that "he was certainly of West's school," presumably referring to his incursions into the field of historical composition, and that "correct in drawing, with a fine manner of composition, and a true eye for light and shadow, he was defective in coloring." His color never achieves the subtlety of Stuart's silver-grays in the "Mrs. Richard Yates," or of the snuff-hued costume of Willson Peale's "Timothy Matlack," however satisfactorily it serves for the artificiality of his characteristic style of portraiture.

Copley's title to the present-day acclaim of him as a master of portrait-painting is anything but justified by the great majority of the likenesses from his easel. It is only in occasional canvases, and when he was forgetful for the moment of his repute for the highly affected sort of thing he commonly contrived, that he succeeded in painting really great portraits. This evaluation of his abilities and accomplishment runs contrary to generally accepted opinion. It is, however, thoroughly considered, and expressed frankly and without reservation in the firm belief that the future will provide all the justification it may seem to lack to-day.

Benjamin West

The first artistic efforts of Benjamin West, outstanding American painter of his time, are associated with his native soil, though for the greater part of his life he made his home in England. Born on a farm in Chester County in the Province of Pennsylvania, in 1738, of humble birth, he was in reality of excellent stock, his forebears, the Wests of Long Crendon in England, being the descendants of Lord Delaware, who participated in the wars of Edward III and the Black Prince. His father and mother were Quakers, but broad-minded enough to countenance and even encourage his childish efforts at picture-making with pen and ink. Indeed, the success of these efforts kindled in his parents a kindly admiration. As a boy, he drew in chalk six heads which he sold to the father of General Anthony Wayne for a dollar apiece. It was very likely this transaction or another similar one that finally induced him to adopt for his livelihood the profession of painter.

West's first colors were charcoal and chalk, mixed with the juices of berries, and his first brushes he made by drawing the hair of the family cat through goose quills. Later he procured from the banks of the Mohawk and the Delaware red and yellow clay, and his mother's indigo pot supplied him with blue. It was with these primitive colors and brushes that his first pictures were painted. Soon thereafter a Philadelphia merchant, who had visited the Wests' home, generously presented the boy with a box of paints and brushes, together with several pieces of canvas. Some of the pictures painted with these colors were exhibited sixty-seven years later in the same room with his famous canvas "Christ Rejected."

In 1756, after the death of his mother, West went to live in Philadelphia with his brother-in-law, and was successfully employed as a portrait-painter in that city, where he acquired something of the facility in execution which became really remarkable in after years. At this period he received a guinea and a half for a head, and five guineas for a half-length. Visiting New York, he pursued his professional career there for eleven months, charging double the prices he had been asking in Philadelphia and accumulating almost enough for his longed for trip abroad. At the age of twenty-one he embarked, reaching Gibraltar safely; and, proceeding up the Mediterranean with some of the officers he met there, he arrived finally in Rome. Here he became overnight the man of the hour, it having been learned that he was an American, neither black nor a savage, but fair, intelligent, and already a painter of some talent.

Four years later he went to London and there began his long career as a painter of historic events. King George III, who was impressed by one of the earliest of these pictures, commissioned him to paint a canvas for the royal collection, and from that time on West was in high favor at court, one entire room at Windsor Castle being given up to the display of his works. He still painted an occasional portrait, but devoted the major portion of his time to the creation of the large historical compositions upon which his fame still rests, realizing fully that in the former field he could not successfully compete with Sir Joshua Reynolds and the other contemporary English masters.

He welcomed to his studio without reservation those American artists who sought his criticism, and virtually all of them he encouraged according to their abilities. Charles Willson Peale, Gilbert Stuart, John Singleton Copley, and John Trumbull—the last-named a pupil for several years in his home—he helped and encouraged. There is not one of these artists but owed something of their skill in after years to the teaching and criticism of the American master in England.

Upon the death of Reynolds, West was chosen

president of the Royal Academy, and upon his election to this office he was offered a knighthood, which he courteously declined. The advice to embryo painters, contained in his inaugural address delivered in March, 1792, has the distinction of being as sound to-day as it was then. He had the gift of plain common sense and of going straight to the heart of a subject without unnecessary digression. The truth of this statement is as evident in his paintings as it is in his discourses. It explains in large measure his achievement as a great painter as well as a great teacher and critic of art.

Though he was commonly spoken of at that time as a Quaker, West was not at all a Quaker in manner, dress, conversation, or conduct. On the contrary, although he was very neat in dress, there was nothing at all of the grave simplicity of that religious sect in his habitual attire—in the powdered curls, the fine linen and garments, such as were worn by all gentlemen. In appearance he was of medium stature, well proportioned and athletic in build, with a fair complexion and piercing eyes.

George III, the artist's patron and friend, died while West himself was confined to his bed with his last sickness. Mrs. West died in December of 1817, and three years later the artist passed away and was buried beside Sir Joshua Reynolds and John Opie in St. Paul's Cathedral.

The particular type of painting which West practised almost to the exclusion of all others has suffered an eclipse in the years since his death, and such huge historic panoramas, which are the evidence of a grasp of dramatic construction beyond the capabilities of the modern artist, have gone entirely out of favor. Fortunately, he found time in the intervals between the painting of these great canvases to do a number of admirable portraits. The likeness of an unknown gentleman, at the Chicago Art Institute, together with the "John Sedley," painted in 1802 and belonging to Mr. Walter Jennings, show how competent he really was as a portrait-painter.

Of West's likenesses, especially of men, it may be said that their suavity as well as their sincerity, their fine color as well as their technical refinement, almost persuade one that he might have excelled in portraiture had he chosen to work in that field of art. At least, his few portraits make one somewhat regret his almost complete absorption in the painting of historic compositions. In the modeling of a head, and in the sensitive emphasis of individual characteristics of expression in a face, he was notably successful.

Charles Willson Peale

Probably the most versatile of our early craftsmen and painters was Charles Willson Peale, who, beginning as an apprentice, pursued the saddler's trade and many others. He attempted coach-making, and later clock- and watch-making, and worked as a silversmith before undertaking portrait- and miniature-painting. In England, later, he made a mezzotint engraving of his half-length of Lord Chatham; there, too, he studied modeling in wax and molding and casting in plaster. His first instructor in portraiture was Gustavus Hesselius, who had married and settled in Annapolis, Maryland, Peale's home.

In 1765, Peale went to Boston and had some criticism and instruction from John Singleton Copley, whose drawing-room he visited. In 1766, with the financial aid of several fellow-citizens of Annapolis, he sailed for London, arriving the next year, and there he studied for about two years with Benjamin

Harvard Law School, Cambridge, Massachusetts

PLATE XIV

THE ROYALL FAMILY

Painted in 1741 by Robert Feke

West, returning in 1769. It was but a short time after his return to America that he came to be generally recognized and appreciated as a portrait-painter.

In 1776, Peale was established in Philadelphia, and as a captain of volunteers saw active service under General Washington at the Battle of Trenton. In 1779 he was a member from Philadelphia of the Pennsylvania Legislature. From that year until 1785 he devoted himself whole-heartedly to portrait-painting, working in oils and also painting miniatures, but from then on much of his time and interest was given up to natural history and the formation of a museum.

His devotion to art had not died, however, and in 1791 he attempted to form an Academy of Fine Arts in Philadelphia. In his old age he was very critical of his earlier works, and distressed by their loss of color in the flesh tints through the use of improper pigments. That the formation of the Pennsylvania Academy of Fine Arts was due to his initiative is concrete evidence of the influence he exerted among the cultivated people in the city of his adoption. William Dunlap, writing in 1834, says that "Peale's works will be soon forgotten"; yet to-day, almost a century later, his portraits are highly valued, and the best of them are respected alike by artists and laymen as works of marked excellence. He is represented in the Metropolitan Museum of Art and the New York Historical Society in New York City.

While in the main Willson Peale's likenesses in oils lack distinction, in several exceptional examples —such as the portrait of his brother James (1749–1831) painting a miniature, owned by Mr. Herbert L. Pratt; that of William Whetcroft, Baltimore silversmith; and that of Timothy Matlack (1736?–1829), a Revolutionary patriot—he created canvases of indubitable artistic merit. The beautifully rendered snuff-colored coat and waistcoat, the finely modeled head, the strongly marked features, and the skilfully interpreted expression in the last-named canvas make it an unforgettable work.

The Whetcroft portrait, belonging to Mr. John Hill Morgan, has every appearance of being a work of similar artistic virtue. The expression in the face is realized with what seems like an effortless translation of significant subtleties too insubstantial to be elucidated in words; it is nevertheless evident in the

Worcester Art Museum, Worcester, Massachusetts

PLATE XV

CORNELIUS WALDO

Painted in 1750 by Joseph Badger

picture, and as obvious to the eye of the layman as to that of the connoisseur of art.

Peale's reputation as a portrait-painter suffers most from the fact that it is based in the main upon his likenesses of George Washington, rather than upon such admirable canvases as those above cited. He signally failed in his portrayals of Washington to express in any sensible degree the force and authority of the military genius, the kindliness of the well-to-do country squire, the courtliness and magnanimity of our first President, or the benignity and serenity of the "father of his country" in the welcome retirement of his last years, spent in unmolested peace on his lovely Mount Vernon farm, the cares of state well past. Peale's pictures of Washington bear virtually no resemblance to any of the many others painted from life, which all reveal well-indicated and perfectly patent similarities in the shape and size of the head, and more particularly in the outline of features; and one is forced to the conclusion that his likenesses in this instance are singularly misleading.

Not only the portraits of Washington by such

artists as Gilbert Stuart, Joseph Wright, and John Trumbull, but the measured and accurate sculptures of Jean Antoine Houdon, which those artists approximate in their drawing, fortify this belief. As a young man, in the beginning of his career as an artist, Peale was anything but skilful in achieving a correct likeness; nor was his color or his technic sufficiently distinguished to compensate for his failure in this respect. As he aged he improved, and some of his later portraits go far toward entitling him to high rank among his contemporaries.

Henry Benbridge

Henry Benbridge was born in Philadelphia. After having studied in Italy in the seventeen-sixties, he painted a portrait of General Pascal Paoli in Corsica in 1768, which was engraved and published in London the following year, with the name "Bembridge" as the painter—an error which for a long time went uncorrected. In 1770 he exhibited at the Royal Academy a likeness of Benjamin Franklin executed in London. Probably late that year he returned to America, bearing a letter from Franklin to his wife which said, "This will be delivered to you by Mr.

Benbridge, who has so greatly improved himself in Italy as a Portrait painter that the connoisseurs here think few or none excel him"—which is pretty strong evidence that the sitter was highly pleased with his likeness by the artist.

Benbridge's large group of "The Gordon Family," probably the first work done by him after his return from abroad, is the most ambitious canvas undertaken by a native artist in Pennsylvania up to the time of its execution, 1771. It is sixty-six inches high by seventy-four inches wide, and is unmistakably Italian in feeling, as is plainly evidenced by the naked "bambino." It also has the brownish hue of Battoni's palette and opaque shadows.

Very soon after the completion of this large canvas, and but little more than a year previous to the death of Jeremiah Theus, Benbridge removed to Charleston, South Carolina. Here he painted numerous portraits which were invariably unsigned and many of which, of women, have been masquerading for untold years as the work of John Singleton Copley. Benbridge painted a number of group portraits, or "conversation pieces" as they were termed, both life-size and in little. Among the latter was one, reputed to be very beautiful, of his sister with her husband, John Saltar, and four children, out of doors; another was of Commodore Truxton and his family. The artist continued to practise in Charleston until about the close of the eighteenth century, when he went to Norfolk, Virginia. At Norfolk he gave Thomas Sully his first lessons in painting in oils.

As a youth in London, Henry Benbridge seems to have had little or no doubt about eventually succeeding in his profession, as he writes home from there, "If I stay here I shall get money fast, or if I should come to America I am not afraid but I shall do well there too." As to his manner of painting, he wrote his mother, "I am not long painting a picture, having studied an expeditious way and at the same time a correct one." Unfortunately, he does not elucidate the details of this expeditious method.

Samuel King

Chiefly because of the fact that he taught Gilbert Stuart, Washington Allston, and Edward Greene Malbone, in their youth, some of the rudiments of art, Charles King deserves recognition to-day. His

Courtesy of the Ehrich Galleries, New York City

PLATE XVI

UNIDENTIFIED LADY

By Jeremiah Theus

oil portraits are less successful than his work in miniature, and would not of themselves entitle him to distinction. In 1771 he painted a canvas of President Stiles of Yale College, having in the previous year done a miniature of him.

King was the teacher of Miss Anne Hall of Connecticut, one of our most proficient native miniaturists. His likeness of Mrs. Richard Derby in oils is reproduced in the Bayley-Goodspeed edition of Dunlap, where three canvases besides the Stiles and Derby portraits are listed.

James Peale

As might be expected of one who was primarily a miniaturist, the best of James Peale's likenesses in oils are small in size and in bust or half-length. His larger oil portraits, such as the Washingtons, were undertaken at the instigation of his elder brother, Charles Willson, who had encouraged him as a young man to give up his trade as a cabinet-maker, and who instructed him in painting in the seventeen-sixties. The small portraits probably represent the artist's personal preference, and are invariably the more successful, though there is enough variation in their quality to substantiate the belief that he worked at a disadvantage in oils. However, he continued to paint likenesses in this medium until at least as late as 1812.

James Peale's best small portrait, that of James Chambers in military uniform, is signed, and dated 1809. It is rather handsome, but markedly exhibits the artist's characteristic fault of narrowing unduly the width of his sitter's shoulders, a fault even more noticeable in some of his miniatures of women. The little oil portrait of General Gist in the Clarke collection, on the other hand, is a poor enough performance to show how hard and unhappy Peale was at times in his oils. The large Washingtons at the Historical Society and the Public Library in New York are very mediocre productions; he failed to instil into them much if anything of the personality of the man.

John Durand

A French Huguenot named Jean Durand settled in Derby, Connecticut, in 1685, and later removed to Milford, in what is now New Haven County, in that State. That John Durand the portrait-painter—two

Thomas B. Clarke Collection

PLATE XVII

THOMAS JOHNSON

Painted in 1768 by John Hesselius

of whose canvases were found in the New Haven Colony Historical Society—was his son, there is but little doubt, for he advertised in New York as early as 1767, three years before the first dated likeness from his hand in Virginia. And though most of his work was done in the latter State, from 1770 to 1782, it seems reasonable to assume that he returned to Milford sometime in 1772 and while there painted the portraits now in New Haven, as there are no portraits in Virginia dated after that year until 1775.

According to Robert Sully, as quoted by William Dunlap, John Durand's works "are hard and dry, but appear to have been good likenesses, with less vulgarity than artists of his calibre generally possess." The variety and definition of character in his faces constitute the chief claim of his portraits to our consideration. Two curious idiosyncrasies identify his likenesses of women—the habit of picturing them habitually with a corsage bouquet, the right hand toying with it, and a four-strand necklace of pearls about the throat.

As he was probably a direct ancestor of Asher Durand, it must have been from him that the latter inherited something at least of his predilection for graphic representation. Asher's father, John, who settled in New Jersey, probably was a son or nephew of the artist. He was somewhat of a craftsman and artist, as well as a shopkeeper, for he is known to have made silver spoons.

Ralph Earl

After painting four Revolutionary views (engraved by Amos Doolittle of New Haven, Connecticut, in 1775) and executing a single large landscape, Ralph Earl devoted the remainder of his life to portraiture. He studied that branch of art under Benjamin West in London, immediately after the independence of the American Colonies was established. He returned from England in 1786, painted a few likenesses in New York, then settled in Connecticut, residing in New Milford for many years before his death, and executing most of his best portraits there.

While Earl's technic has little or nothing of individuality, he created a definitely personal type of portrait, painting his sitters almost invariably seated beside a window through which one gets a welcome glimpse of the landscape without. Many of his faces are accurate transcripts, it seems, of those of his sitters, and character is the dominant note in them, revealing with remarkable vigor the personalities portrayed. One is gratified to observe in these portraits a faithful incorporation of detail which helps one to visualize the interiors of the houses of the period as they existed in this country—the customary appearance of the inside of an American home in the seventeen-nineties. The artist is just as precise in his rendering of all the particulars of dress and toilet, the laces and caps of women, and the buckles and waistcoats of men; so that the picture one gets of the time, in looking at a likeness from his easel, is almost as complete as it is perfect.

Admirable examples of Ralph Earl's portraiture may be seen at the Historical Society of New Milford, Connecticut. He is also well represented at the Art Museum of Worcester, Massachusetts, the Metropolitan Museum of Art in New York, and the Chicago Art Institute. Virtually all of his later works are both signed and dated.

Adolph Ulrich Wertmuller

A member of the Royal Academy of Paris and that of Stockholm, Adolph Ulrich Wertmuller came to the United States in 1794, landing in Philadelphia, and painted President Washington in that city the next year. He failed at that time to obtain commissions sufficient to justify his remaining in this country, and returned to Stockholm in 1796, where he resided for several years. Misfortune pursued him there, however, and after losing a large sum in the failure of a mercantile house in Sweden he returned to America in 1800, married in 1801 a granddaughter of Gustavus Hesselius, an earlier Swedish portrait-painter in this country, and settled here permanently.

Wertmuller's likeness of Washington is without evidence of illuminating exposition of personality as indicated by feature or expression, and his portrait of Andrew Hamilton is no less prosaic and literal in its portrayal. The self-portrait, reproduced in the Bayley-Goodspeed edition of Dunlap, is decidedly superior to either of the canvases above mentioned; but the finest work from his hand which I have seen is the likeness of an unknown man, painted in Rome.

John Johnston

The son of a shopkeeper in Brattle Street, Boston, who sold colors, painted coats of arms, engraved portraits, etc., John Johnston, born in 1752, adopted the profession of portrait-painter as a means of livelihood, making likenesses both in pastel and in oils.

Johnston served in the Revolution, reaching the rank of major, and was an original member of the Order of the Cincinnati. The portrait of John Peck, the Boston ship-builder, in the Clarke collection, is an excellent example of his work in oils, and the likeness of C. P. Smith is a fine specimen of his work in crayons. In the latter picture the rich-brown coat, light-brown waistcoat, white ruffled cuffs and stock, together with the subject's white wig, fair complexion, and light-blue eyes, against the dark-gray background, constitute an admirable color ensemble. Johnston appears to have had a true aptitude for securing a good likeness, and in the presence of his pictures one feels the accuracy of his portraiture.

Gilbert Stuart

Our greatest portrait-painter, Gilbert Stuart, was the son of a Scotchman who came here about 1750 and put up a snuff-mill near Narragansett, Rhode Island. The boy was capable and strong-willed and, being an only son, was naturally allowed to have pretty much his own way. Dr. Benjamin Waterhouse, a boyhood friend, says that Stuart began copying pictures when about thirteen and very soon thereafter tried likenesses in black lead.

His father moved to Newport from Narragansett, and it was in the latter town that young Stuart, in the early seventeen-seventies, came under the tutelage of Cosmo Alexander, another Sotchman, who was something of a portrait-painter, from whom he learned a little of drawing and how to make up his palette.

With Alexander, Stuart went to South Carolina and thence to Scotland, where he was virtually destitute after the death of his mentor and that of a friend in whose care Alexander left him. Stuart managed to get back across the Atlantic by working his passage on a collier which landed him in Nova Scotia. From there he tramped back to Newport, save for such "lifts" as he got from good-natured farmers, arriving dirty and in rags.

No sooner was the young artist cleaned up and in

a new suit of clothes, however, than he went to painting again. It was then that he and Benjamin Waterhouse drew from life a muscular blacksmith, who posed for them for a half-dollar an evening. Waterhouse says that Stuart even at that time was aware of the great importance of drawing with anatomical correctness, and made every effort to perfect himself in that art.

One of the first portraits painted by Gilbert Stuart after his return from abroad was a likeness, from memory, of his mother, who had died about ten years before. It was this likeness that brought about his recognition as a portrait-painter. Joseph Anthony of Philadelphia, his mother's brother, was so impressed by this canvas that he employed his nephew to paint his likeness, his wife's, and thereafter the likenesses of their two children. Another man of wealth followed Anthony's example, and the painter was finally established professionally.

It is recorded that at this time the buoyancy of Stuart's spirits kept pace with his good fortune. It did not continue to do so, however. The self-portrait of 1778, in the Redwood Library at Newport, plainly reveals the temperamental disposition of the young genius, and one can confidently assume that his reputation as a man of uneven temper, either at the top of his form or in the depths of despondency, is entirely justified.

At the age of twenty-four Stuart was in London, and Benjamin West, learning from some one of his straitened circumstances, sent a message to him, with several guineas and an invitation to call. This generosity and kindliness Stuart always appreciated, writing later that "on application to receive me as a pupil, I was welcomed with true benevolence, encouraged and taken into the family . . . Nothing could exceed the attentions of that artist to me; they were paternal." He was soon established as one of the leading portrait-painters in London, getting as much for his work as any other with the exception of Reynolds, and his pictures hung in the best lights and the most conspicuous places at the Royal Academy exhibitions.

Received everywhere as a man of mark, Gilbert Stuart might have become famous and wealthy, except for the fact that his indulgences and improvidence estranged the powerful personages who would have been his friends. He lived in splendor and with

Detroit Institute of Arts, Detroit, Michigan

PLATE XVIII

CLARA WALKER ALLEN

By John Woolaston

a gaiety somewhat artificially contrived, at one time the host of a brilliant salon and at another languishing in a debtor's prison. John Trumbull, indeed, encountered him at West's house, in 1780, dressed in an old black coat, torn at the hip and pinned up, and looking, as Trumbull said, "more like a poor beggar than a painter."

In 1794, Stuart returned home from England, with the idea in the back of his mind of painting President Washington. On his arrival in the United States, he occupied a studio on Stone Street in New York City for several months, where he painted a number of likenesses, some astonishingly beautiful, others decidedly mediocre, in the manner of a man who is either at his best or sunk in spirit. His first portrait of Washington (the Vaughn picture) was painted in Philadelphia in 1795, when the President was sixty-three, and is unquestionably the most truthful as well as by far the best of all the portraits from Stuart's brush. The finest of those the artist painted of the popular Athenæum type is the one on a grained wooden panel, which was sold in New York in 1924.

The Lee-Phillips picture of the Vaughn type, reproduced as the frontispiece of this volume, is possibly Stuart's last portrait of Washington from life, and probably was painted in 1797 or 1798. It is the final idealization of the artist's favorite subject, realized in a face tranquil and benign, lightened by an expression of gentle cheerfulness, very ingratiating in effect. The coloring is surprisingly fresh and clear; the drawing, especially of the jabot, which is done with a minimum of realism, very fine indeed; the modeling of the head accurate, and the rendering of the expression in the countenance managed without sign of effort, as if it had transpired naturally and unconsciously as the artist proceeded with his work.

In the field of American painting the lack of authoritative criticism, especially as it relates to early portraiture, is nowhere more conspicuous than in the present disagreement among so-called experts regarding Stuart's likenesses of Washington. Unhappily, the qualifications of the majority of these critics do not include any first-hand knowledge of the technic of painting, or even a really cultivated appreciation of artistic values of a personal and individual sort. Some base their judgments upon

Property of Mrs. George S. Winslow

PLATE XIX

THE WINSLOW FAMILY

By Joseph Blackburn

similarities of drawing as shown in features or costume, others upon references found in records of earlier days and the *provenance* of a picture. Both methods are notoriously inconclusive in many instances.

As a result of such muddled, arbitrary, and inconclusive opinion, there exists to-day a discrepancy almost insuperable, not only concerning the authenticity of some of these portraits, but with regard to the priority and merit of others which all critics acknowledge. Portraits for which a record has been provided in very recent years, and which have no credible *provenance* at all, are passed by some, who at the same time disqualify others much finer in themselves and more in Stuart's manner, which have unassailable histories dating back to the beginning of the last century.

One of these self-styled experts has but recently mistakenly based his adverse opinion of an exceptionally fine portrait of the Vaughn type upon the misunderstanding that six portraits of Washington were painted in 1797 or 1798 for Martha Washington, from a miniature. This idea he may have derived from Miss Johnson's "Original Portraits of Washington," a book containing many errors, which has long been discounted as being in any sense authoritative. As a matter of fact, the six portraits of Washington referred to by Miss Johnson, which the "expert" cites, were miniatures painted by Robert Field, after Washington's death, for Mrs. Washington. They are all listed and described in Mr. Harry Piers's comprehensive work on Field.

Other "experts" dispute the priority of the Vaughn portrait itself, a matter established beyond the shadow of a doubt by records, history, and the testimony of Rembrandt Peale, who saw it while Stuart was working upon it and afterward while it was in the possession of Joseph Harrison of Philadelphia, who had purchased it in England in 1851 from the Vaughn family, and from whose estate Mr. Clarke bought it.

Innumerable instances of just such mistaken judgment and incomprehensible substitution of personal prejudice for clear thinking and scientific study might be cited.

The notion that Gilbert Stuart ever referred to his Washington portraits as his "hundred-dollar pictures," in the sense of turning out one for that sum whenever he was in need of funds, is as absurd as the story of George Washington and the cherry tree, and may be quite as hard to kill. The great majority of the inferior portraits of both the Vaughn and Athenæum types were painted by other artists, contemporary and of later date, and not by Stuart himself. The number of them which has been placed in American collections through the connivance of these same "experts" is more damning to their pretenses than all that they have ever said or written on the subject.

No English portrait from Stuart's hand is more satisfying than the "Ozias Humphrey" in the Wadsworth Athenæum at Hartford, Connecticut. Very directly done, it has all the charm of a picture painted *con amore* and almost at a single sitting. The excellent "Caleb Whitefoord," a more colorful work, approaches more nearly the slight artificiality of the English portraiture of its day. Of the American works, other than the Washingtons, invariably the less studied, more sketch-like, and sometimes partly unfinished likenesses are the most lovely of all—portraits like the "Mrs. Robert Morris" at the New York Public Library and the "Mrs. Perez Morton" at the Art Museum in Worcester, Massachusetts. They are just so much the more marvelous as portraits for their utter simplicity—appealing because of the charm or character of the sitter alone, unenforced by fetching pose or fine costuming. While many of Stuart's portraits are decidedly of the English school rather than the American, one finds the unaffectedness of the latter in a few; and these few rank with the best of his works.

Gilbert Stuart painted Sir Joshua Reynolds, but not to that artist's satisfaction; and, for all his study of drawing, he was not in his day thought of as a great draftsman in any sense. Stuart built up a reputation for portraiture which ranks him with the greatest, a more than slight overestimate of his abilities. This reputation probably was based upon the fundamentals of painting as gathered from the advice and example of his "good old master" West. He never described the course of study recommended by West, but said that facility and accuracy of execution were required—a faithful representation of some object casually presented to the eye.

Stuart used a small oval palette, and, according to

Pennsylvania Academy of Fine Arts, Philadelphia

PLATE XX

BENJAMIN WEST

By Matthew Pratt

Dunlap, arranged the colors thereon thus: first, nearest the thumb, pure white; then vermilion, black, and blue, followed by yellow and white in gradation; vermilion and white in gradation; black and yellow; black and vermilion; black and white; blue and white, and—for finishing—lake and asphaltum. Later he used Antwerp blue, Krem's white, vermilion, stone-ochre, lake, vandyke brown mixed with one third burnt umber, and ivory black. The tints he mixed were white and yellow; vermilion and white; white, yellow, and vermilion; vermilion and lake; blue and white, black and yellow; black, vermilion, and lake. When asked if he used madder-lake, his reply was, "I should be madder if I did." The flesh tints in faces he almost invariably painted in vermilion, but lips he often painted in madder (not madder-lake), and these have discolored, as in many of the Washingtons, from the action of the white-lead under-painting.

Before drawing in a likeness, it was Stuart's habit to observe which side of the face gave the better outline of the nose, and to choose this as the side nearer the spectator's eye. He always held that likeness depended more upon the nose than upon any other feature. Most of his pictures, he failed to sign, but he said that he "marked them all over."

Joseph Wright

The bust portrait of General Washington in profile painted by Joseph Wright at Rocky Hill, New Jersey, in 1783, and now in the Cleveland Museum of Art, is the most faithful likeness we have in oils. It is also the one General Washington himself preferred.

Joseph Wright was the son of Patience Wright, celebrated as a modeler in wax, and was born at Bordentown, New Jersey, in 1756. Taken to London by his mother in 1772, after his father's death, he studied with Benjamin West and with John Hoppner, who married Wright's sister, and he had already become a recognized portrait-painter there, and had executed a likeness of George IV as Prince of Wales, before leaving England in 1782.

In Paris, whither the artist now went, he did a bust of Franklin, under whose protection his mother had placed him; and in October of 1782 he departed for America. After painting General Washington

Pennsylvania Academy of Fine Arts, Philadelphia

PLATE XXI

MRS. BENJAMIN WEST

By Matthew Pratt

and Mrs. Washington at Rocky Hill, he practised in Philadelphia, where he painted the small group of himself and his family which is now at the Pennsylvania Academy of Fine Arts in that city, and a likeness of James Madison. He also practised in New York for a time, and while there he did the portrait of a Jewish gentleman named Simpson, a picture very highly praised by Dunlap.

John Trumbull

In his finer bust and full-length portraits, John Trumbull compares very favorably with the best of his contemporaries. As a matter of fact, his full-length of President Washington done in 1792, now in the Yale Art Gallery, is preferable to Gilbert Stuart's Landsdowne or Dorchester Heights pictures.

The customary criticism of this work by Trumbull—that it represents Washington not as he appeared when it was painted but as he looked some years before—carries very little weight. Trumbull's acquaintance with his subject was a matter of seventeen years' standing when this picture was begun: he had served on the general's staff as early as 1775, and the relationship had long before culminated in a personal friendship which gave the artist unusual facilities for memorizing Washington's appearance. It is more than probable, therefore, that the likeness here is quite as accurate as that in any of Stuart's canvases. That it represents the subject at an earlier date than the canvas was painted is a matter of no moment whatever, for the fact does not at all detract from the validity of the picture as a work of art.

Trumbull's bust portrait of Mrs. Lenox, at the New York Public Library, is an almost completely satisfying symphony, blond in tone and beautiful in its rendition of a music high in key in a muted minor strain. It suggests Gilbert Stuart's "Mrs. Richard Yates," one of the masterpieces of our greatest portrait-painter. In this size, Trumbull's pictures of Mr. and Mrs. Stephen Minott which hang in the Boston Museum, his "Asher B. Durand" owned by the New York Historical Society, and the self-portrait in the Yale Art Gallery, together with the likeness already cited, make a really impressive group. One could form an imaginary grouping of his full-lengths—the "Washington" of 1792, "General Morgan Lewis," "Governor Clinton," and "Governor Tompkins" at the City Hall in New York

City—which would surpass in general effectiveness any group of similar portraits painted by an American artist.

Trumbull had the invaluable power of incorporating in the faces of his sitters characteristics of expression, and of emphasizing just those peculiar dissimilarities of feature that make the impression of a person's individuality as it is revealed in his appearance. On the other hand, this artist is not a great virtuoso of the brush, and his technic conforms to the academic style of his day. Color contributes to the success of his portraits more by chance than by design, but it is color unlighted by the fire of genius, and, however effective, it fails to glorify his canvases as does the color of Stuart when that artist is at his best.

The huge compositions undertaken by Trumbull for Congress have been much criticized. It is maintained, and rightly, that he was incapable of achieving a proper effect in canvases of such magnitude. It seems to be forgotten, however, that the choice of subjects and size was left to President Madison; and that it was the President who insisted upon their being twelve feet high by eighteen wide, with figures the size of life, whereas the artist had wished to paint them exactly half that size. Surely, all the blame for their failure in an artistic sense should not be charged to Trumbull. The grandiloquent statement of C. Edwards Lester concerning these compositions is one of the outstanding curiosities of the criticism of his time. He wrote of them in 1846:

> Congress paid grudgingly $8000 a piece for his four great Paintings in the Rotunda—but what Representative of the American people would dare now to rise in his place and propose to *sell* the Declaration of Independence, I care not what sum were offered for it? It is the only Picture in the world which has preserved the forms and the expressions of the great fathers of American Liberty—and it would be sacrilege to ruin it, because it is above all price.

Born June 6, 1756, in Lebanon, Connecticut, the youngest child of Jonathan Trumbull, Revolutionary governor of that State, John Trumbull was a descendant of the Puritans on both his father's and his mother's side. His father was born in Lebanon in 1710, and his mother's ancestors had come to this country as early as 1620. As a child John made crude attempts at drawing on the sanded floors of his home, but he maintained in after years that what we are too ready to ascribe to natural genius in the young is more often merely a natural aptitude for imitation. At sixteen he went to Harvard College, and while there endeavored in vain to persuade his father to permit him to study with John Singleton Copley, then the foremost portrait-painter in Boston. Undiscouraged, he studied such paintings and prints as he encountered, and made many drawings, besides two copies in color of an Italian picture of Mount Vesuvius.

From 1775 to 1777 Trumbull served in the Continental Army, first as adjutant of a regiment, later as aide-de-camp to General Washington and deputy-adjutant to General Gates. By the end of 1779 he had managed to paint sixty-eight pictures, though he had received no instruction except from books and the study of paintings he saw.

In 1780, Trumbull sailed from New London, Connecticut, to France, and proceeded from there to London. He was apprehended and imprisoned in England for high treason, and it was in this extremity that Benjamin West interceded with the king in his behalf and eventually managed to secure his freedom. Returning home immediately thereafter, he again sailed for England in 1783, arriving in January of the year following and remaining abroad until 1789, most of the time studying under West, who in 1780 had said to him, "I have now no hesitation to say that nature intended you for a painter."

After 1789, Trumbull began the series of full-lengths for the Corporation of the City of New York and, with digressions consequent upon commissions elsewhere, continued to practise there until the end of 1808. From 1816 to the time of his death in 1843 he had many pupils, and exercised with unremitting zeal his interest in art, completing a number of pictures despite accumulating infirmities. He died in New York City, and is buried beside his wife in New Haven, Connecticut, where he founded at Yale the first college art museum in America.

Samuel Broadbent

Dr. Samuel Broadbent, of Wethersfield, Connecticut, born March 29, 1759, is to be numbered among the hitherto unrecorded New England portrait-painters of the late eighteenth century. He painted a number of likenesses that are deserving of the attention of students of early native portraiture. The companion pictures of John Churchill (1785–1823), and his wife, Laura Wells Churchill (1789–1873), owned by Mr. George Dudley Seymour of New Haven, Connecticut, were painted probably in Wethersfield in 1813. Churchill is described as a man of medium stature, slender build, and quiet manner; a farmer, but evidently a cultivated man. That he was successful and well-to-do is evidenced by the manner in which his wife dressed.

In the same way as Ralph Earl, Samuel Broadbent reproduces with meticulous care laces, ribbons, and jewelry, and contents himself with securing a likeness of his subject, without enough of expression to indicate individual character. A distinguishing feature of his likenesses is the eye, in which alone he was able to indicate a little of the personality of a sitter. In some instances his faces are broken up by deep furrows and hard lines, much in the same manner as those of Richard Jennys and other of our early portraitists whose lack of training rendered them incapable of softening the evidences of age and trouble to any degree approximating its inconspicuousness in the interplay of emotion, as in the living countenance.

Color, in any real sense, Broadbent's portraits generally lack. In pose his sitters are noticeably erect. As a draftsman this artist had no more than ordinary ability, and with hands, which are most often the despair and undoing of the portrait-painter, he was notoriously unsuccessful—though he attempted an exceedingly difficult one in the portrait of John Churchill.

Considering the fact that Broadbent was a provincial painter of local reputation only, presumably self-taught and practising art probably only as a diversion from the professional duties of a country physician, his success in the field of portraiture is really remarkable. It is unlikely that he found opportunity for painting many portraits, and unquestionably but few of his works are preserved.

James Sharples

The small pastel portraits, especially those in profile, painted in this country by the English artist James Sharples, between 1796 and 1811, were highly thought of at the time and are even more highly valued to-day. Customarily about six by nine inches in size, they are exquisitely finished to the last de-

Yale Art Gallery, New Haven, Connecticut

PLATE XXII

EZRA STILES

By Nathaniel Smibert

tail, accurately drawn, and colored with consummate skill. The artist visited virtually every town of importance in the United States, producing innumerable likenesses of distinguished men of the time, charging twenty dollars for portraits in full-face and fifteen for those in profile, and eventually accumulated a modest fortune. In New England particularly there must be dozens of unrecorded works from his hand.

Sharples's portraits of George and Martha Washington are among the first of those he painted in America. The popularity of his likeness of the former resulted in his making upward of thirty replicas—in which, it is true, one notes variations, but variations that are unimportant. His likeness of our first President is still ranked to-day, as it was in 1796, when it was painted, next to Stuart's portraits of the Vaughn and Athenæum types. The portraits in oil which Sharples is reputed to have done have, it seems, disappeared. William Dunlap, who mentions having seen one of his pictures in that medium, intimates that the artist was more successful in his work with crayons.

The fact that his wife and his sons, James and

Felix, all painted portraits in the style he made his own, copying many from his originals, testifies to the popularity of his product. He was partial to blue, and that color is characteristic of his portraiture, though oftener than not it is modified by gray or some other suitable hue. In the purely linear sense he was an accomplished draftsman, but in modeling, as in reproducing the contour of a face, he was less successful, and for that reason his profiles are much better than the likenesses in full-face. His portraits are hardly searching characterizations of his sitters, but one feels that they are accurate if perhaps uninspired representations. Their perennial appeal has more to do with inherent artistic perfection, the result of his remarkable command of an elusive and highly attractive medium, than with resemblance, which is the basic necessity of successful portraiture.

Pastels by Sharples of many notable Americans may be seen at Independence Hall in Philadelphia, and he is represented also in the permanent collections of the Art Museum of Worcester, Massachusetts, the American Antiquarian Society in Worcester, the Metropolitan Museum of Art in New York City, the Manor Hall at Yonkers, New York, and the

Hartford Athenæum, Hartford, Connecticut

PLATE XXIII

MRS. SEYMOUR FORT

By John Singleton Copley

Wadsworth Athenæum in Hartford, Connecticut, which owns fine examples of his George and Martha Washington portraits.

Edward Savage

The reputation of Edward Savage as a portrait-painter rests chiefly upon the large group of "General Washington and His Family," painted from life between 1789 and 1796 in New York and Philadelphia. This huge canvas, eighty-four inches high by one hundred and eleven inches wide, from which the artist made an engraving that had a wide sale, was also reproduced both in black-and-white and in colors by a number of publishers, but the copies in color never duplicated or even approached the coloring of the original painting.

Savage, who was born in Princeton, Worcester County, Massachusetts, in 1761, was originally a goldsmith. He was commissioned by Harvard College in 1789 to paint the portrait of General Washington now hanging in the art gallery of the university. An inartistic and unsatisfactory canvas, it seems to be the first of his likenesses in oils. In 1791 he went to London, studied with Benjamin West, and visited Italy, returning to the United States in 1794. The next year he exhibited in Philadelphia the first panorama ever shown in that city, representing London and Westminster. William Dunlap belittles his work by quoting David Edwin the engraver as saying, "I do not wish the credit which is to be derived from pictures of Mr. Savage's composition," and states that the son of John Wesley Jarvis contended he soon found he could paint better than his master (Savage) and engrave ten times better. How much of this is truth and how much is inspired by professional jealousy on their part or Dunlap's, the reader may readily judge from an inspection of Savage's portraiture, such as the miniature of himself in the Art Museum in Worcester, Massachusetts, the unsatisfactory "Washington" at Harvard University, the large Washington family group in the Clarke collection, and his engravings of the latter, of Willson Peale's "David Rittenhouse," and of the portrait of General Knox.

Mather Brown

There is one American portrait-painter, a contemporary of Gilbert Stuart, whose best work challenges comparison with the portraiture of that master. Mather Brown, who is too little known to-day, was a painter of exceptional ability, and produced, particularly in his early years in London, a number of likenesses which might be hung beside Stuart's without detriment to their merit. Indeed, some of these portraits have since been attributed to Stuart, by recognized authorities.

In the beginning, Brown's portraits were of the American school, natural in pose, simple in style, and significant in expression. In color they were conspicuously refined, his brush-work careful yet free, and the quality of his technic very superior. The early self-portrait illustrates perhaps as well as any of his likenesses the characteristics which identify his portraiture with the American school. Its relationship to the West portraits by Matthew Pratt and its descent from the Thomas Child likeness is perfectly evident even in the reproductions presented in this volume.

Except for a brief period of popularity during his first years in London, in the seventeen-eighties, Brown never enjoyed the recognition he deserved, though a letter written in 1789 and quoted by

Dunlap, says that he "is in the highest state of success, keeps a servant in livery and is appointed portrait painter to the Duke of York and has painted a great many of the nobility and also the Prince of Wales." He was then still under thirty. When a mere lad of sixteen he had begun his career as an artist in America, and by the time he was twenty had prospered sufficiently to permit of his going abroad with ample means in hand for his support for three years.

Arriving in Paris with a letter to Benjamin Franklin, Brown proceeded to London, where in 1781 he studied with Benjamin West, and the following year showed his first picture, a portrait, at the Royal Academy. Success seems to have turned his head. He took a fine apartment, began to live beyond his means, and as a final consequence, harassed by debt, he became moody and uncivil to a degree that alienated friends and discouraged custom. He never returned to the United States, and few if any of the portraits he painted in this country as a youth, previous to his departure in 1780, are known to-day. After practising his profession for almost half a

In private possession

PLATE XXIV

HENRY PELHAM

(Boy with the Squirrel)
By John Singleton Copley

century in England, exhibiting a total of eighty pictures at the Royal Academy, he died in 1831.

Robert Fulton

Probably the earliest instruction in art Robert Fulton had was from the study of the works of Charles Willson Peale, the principal painter in Philadelphia in the seventeen-eighties. He began painting landscapes and portraits in 1782, when he was seventeen years old, and managed by his diligence and economy to purchase, when twenty-one, a little farm in Pennsylvania for his mother. Having accomplished that, he sailed for London, where he became the pupil of Benjamin West. The American master appreciated the young artist enough to paint his portrait and to present him with a portrait of himself. It was while on this visit to England that Fulton renewed his interest in mechanics, which later led him to forsake art for invention and it was there that he constructed the first submarine. The idea that Fulton invented the steamboat, though rather widespread, is entirely erroneous, though the operation of his *Clermont* between New York and Albany was the beginning of steam navigation as a commercial success.

In 1794, Fulton discontinued practice as a portrait-painter, though he still painted an occasional likeness, such as the full-lengths of his friend Henry Eckford (1775–1832) and of Mrs. Eckford, both of 1809. He also painted, in 1814, Mahlon Dickerson (1770–1853); and, in 1800, Charlotte Villette. The life-size Eckford pictures are sincere and dignified works of considerable merit, with a depth and richness of coloring well calculated to throw into relief the finely modeled heads and emphasize the expression in the faces. As a young man Fulton made a number of miniatures, and in after years he drew in pencil for his friend Eckford a self-portrait which is perhaps as good as anything he ever did in oils. It is a straightforward study, without evidence of an artist's customary habit of trying to improve upon nature when it comes to painting or drawing his own likeness.

William Dunlap

As a lad of seventeen, William Dunlap made an early full-length likeness of General Washington at

Property of Mr. Walter Jennings, New York

PLATE XXV

JOHN SEDLEY

Painted in 1802 by Benjamin West

Rocky Hill, New Jersey, but the artist himself ascribes his first portrait in oils—undertaken for the assistance of a sign-painter—to 1782, the preceding year. In 1784 he went to England, where he studied under Robert Davey, who had been taught in Rome, and during that year and the next received a few lessons from Benjamin West, copying one or two of West's compositions.

During his stay in England, Dunlap attempted several pictures which he never managed to finish, a group of Captain Lawrence's boys and some more elaborate historical pictures. He did, however, complete a few portraits, one of which West criticized rather severely, though Dunlap says that "it was freely touched, well colored, and full of expression." He seems to have led in London the easy life of a youth given by his parents every advantage in preparing himself for an artistic career.

Finally, in 1787, Dunlap embarked for home, and arrived in the United States after a long passage of seven weeks, during which he painted two likenesses of the captain of the ship. Between 1789 and 1805 he became much interested in literary and theatrical affairs, and painted but a few somewhat sketchy portraits and some miniatures, mostly of rather inferior quality. In 1813 and 1814 he was again painting portraits in oils—as he says, "with a success beyond my expectation." Several huge religious subjects completed in the years following were exhibited with more or less success in many of our large cities, and were variously estimated by artists and the public. It is safe to assume that, whatever their success at the time, they were pretty impossible as works of art. The painter himself says that he had a better eye for form than for color, and he certainly was not a great draftsman.

Dunlap's rank as an artist is not accurately reflected by the many pages devoted to his autobiography in the "History of the Arts of Design." The publication of that first comprehensive survey of American art is a better monument to his memory than any picture he ever painted. His "History of the American Theatre" also is an indispensable source-book in another field.

Ezra Ames

Beginning as a coach-painter in Albany, New York, Ezra Ames in the early years of the nineteenth century graduated to portrait-painting. Two of his early likenesses were those of Governor George Clinton and Alexander Hamilton, painted from life. He later painted many of the Western members of the legislature, before retiring on an income derived from savings, the result of his unflagging industry and frugality.

Richard Jennys

Richard Jennys, an English engraver and painter, emigrated to America, probably landing in Boston late in the eighteenth century. Contrary to Dunlap's statement, he did not reside in Boston altogether, however, for in 1783 he advertised in South Carolina as recently arrived from the North, and the following year again as continuing the business of portrait-painting, chiefly in miniature—the only record we have of his practising that branch of portraiture.

Following his sojourn in the South, Jennys must have practised for a year or so in the vicinity of New Milford, Connecticut, where some time ago were discovered the only signed and dated portraits from his hand so far recorded. These works, representing Isaac Hawley and his wife Tamar, are dated 1798.

Since this discovery, there have been found in New Milford seven additional likenesses from his hand. That of Ithamar Canfield, reproduced in this volume, is a typical example—hard in a linear sense, unprepossessing in color, but withal a surprisingly impressive canvas, acquainting one with a distinct personality. Jennys had a habit of close observation which enabled him to picture his sitters with rather remarkable fidelity, and it is this fact that has so far served to save his portraiture from the oblivion that eventually engulfs the merely commonplace.

In his portraiture the emphasis is entirely upon variation of features and form and the habitual expression of the sitter. His abilities do not extend to the subtleties that mark the works of greater artists with distinction. His line is hard, if true, and his coloring misses the variability of tone and value that intrigues the eye. His portraits of Lieutenant Elisha Bostwick (1748–1834), a notable Revolutionary soldier, Betty Bostwick, Elisha's wife, and their two children, Jared and Betty Ann, are in the permanent collection of the Historical Society of New Milford, Connecticut.

In Boston he appears to have worked mostly as an

engraver, though the mezzotint of the Rev. Jonathan Mayhew was from a painting by himself. That of Nathaniel Hurd the silversmith was from a protrait by John Singleton Copley. Before his departure from Boston he was, for a time at least, a dealer in dry goods, though there is no record of his remaining in that city after 1777.

Henry Sargent

As a youth Henry Sargent showed no interest whatever in art; after leaving school he entered a counting-house first, and later worked in his father's mercantile establishment, remaining in the latter place until he was nineteen or twenty. His earliest recognition as an artist was by John Trumbull, who saw his work in Boston in 1790.

Three years after this, Sargent went to England and resided for four years in London in the vicinity of Benjamin West's studio, returning to Boston in 1797 and in 1799 entering the United States Army, in which he became a colonel. In England both West and John Singleton Copley were helpful to him, and it was perhaps the success of the former, if not the general popularity of such works at the time, that induced him to devote a great part of his energies to the painting of large historical compositions, such as "Christ Entering Jerusalem," the "Landing of the Pilgrims," and others. Some of his portraits—for example, that of General Benjamin Lincoln (1733–1810), owned by the Massachusetts Historical Society of Boston, that of Mr. Faneuil, and the lovely small one of Sarah Anne St. John (1794–1845)—go far toward persuading us that his proper métier was that of portrait-painting.

John Rubens Smith

John Rubens Smith, the son of John Raphael Smith, an English engraver of conspicuous ability, came to the United States about 1810. He painted small portraits in both water-color and oil in Boston, Philadelphia, and New York, and died in the last-named city in 1849. He was an engraver as well as a painter. His portraiture is of the obviously uninspired type that admits of no comment.

John Vanderlyn

As a youth, John Vanderlyn worked for a time with a print-dealer in New York City and it was there that he developed his taste for art. There, also, he met Gilbert Stuart upon the latter's return from Europe, and copied some of Stuart's portraits. Soon thereafter, in Kingston, New York, his birthplace, Vanderlyn began the practice of portraiture as a profession. For several months he studied with Stuart in Philadelphia; went abroad in 1796, after painting a number of likenesses in New York; returned in 1801, and went again in 1803, when he remained for two years in Paris.

In 1805, Vanderlyn made a tour of the important Italian cities, returning to Paris in 1808. It was in that city, in 1812, that he painted his most celebrated picture, the "Ariadne," which was later purchased and engraved by a fellow-countryman and portrait-painter, Asher B. Durand, whose replica of the picture in oil may be seen at the Metropolitan Museum of Art in New York City. This picture, after more than a century, remains the finest nude so far painted by an American.

For a number of years subsequent to 1817, Vanderlyn undertook the exhibition, in New York City, of certain panoramas, including his own "Versailles." His reputation for portraiture suffers considerably from the fact that his likenesses vary greatly in quality; and yet, though the "Ariadne" remains his greatest picture, he was primarily a portrait-painter. Among the important men of his day of whom he made likenesses were President Monroe and President Madison, Governor Clinton, General Jackson, Vice-President Calhoun, Colonel Mercer, and Albert Gallatin. He seldom, if ever, painted a woman's portrait.

As to the contention that Vanderlyn was a better artist than John Trumbull—in the narrow sense of his having been a better technician, perhaps he was, but in the broader sense he certainly was not.

Jacob Eichholtz

The best portrait-painter of Pennsylvania, Jacob Eichholtz, was born in Lancaster, in that province, in 1776, and his first instruction in art was received from an ordinary sign-painter. Later, apprenticed to a coppersmith, he pictured in charcoal, on the walls of the shop, many of his fellow-workers. He spent his early life as a coppersmith, and was a man of family with several children before he found courage to turn from trade to art as a means of livelihood. He

Property of Mr. John Hill Morgan, New York City

PLATE XXVI

WILLIAM WHETCROFT

By Charles Willson Peale

made a trip to Boston, with his portrait of Nicholas Biddle, which he took as a specimen of his work, to show Gilbert Stuart. Eichholtz tells us that his picture was placed by that artist beside one of his—Stuart's—own, and that he considered that lesson the best he was ever given.

Stuart gave Eichholtz valuable advice and inspired him with confidence. Leaving Boston, the ex-coppersmith moved his family to Philadelphia, where he practised painting successfully for ten years. He was unpretentious, frank, and sensible, and it is safe to surmise that his personal qualities had much to do with his popularity as a portraitist.

Thomas Sully, who for a time painted in the studio of Eichholtz in Lancaster, and in return gave him such professional information as he could, wrote that at that time his comrade's attempts at painting were hideous. A few years later, after the visit to Gilbert Stuart, Sully was surprised at the progress Eichholtz had made, and wrote that he then had no doubt his friend would have made a first-rate painter if he had begun early in life.

As a matter of fact, the portraiture of Eichholtz is decidedly superior to that of Sully. His heads are finely modeled and solidly painted, his faces illuminated with feeling beautifully expressed. His figures are naturally posed and convey an impression of reality which is in direct contrast to the artificiality of too much of the portraiture of his day. Compared with the unaffected charm of his likeness of Mrs. Phœbe Freeman, Thomas Sully's portrait of Mrs. Edward Hudson sinks to the level of a consciously contrived prettiness too obvious for words.

Rembrandt Peale

Both Raphael, the first son, and Rembrandt, the second son, of Charles Willson Peale became portrait-painters. The latter, Rembrandt Peale, lived to be eighty-two years old and produced a great number of likenesses, the best of which deserve more attention than they now receive. His reputation suffers from being too generally based upon his portrait of George Washington than upon his other more successful works. Certainly his "Jacques Louis David" and the "Jean Antoine Houdon" at the Pennsylvania Academy in Philadelphia are far finer than his "Washington," and, furthermore, are portraits of real distinction and superior artistic excellence, ad-

Property of Mr. John Hill Morgan, New York City

PLATE XXVII

MAJOR RICHARD STOCKTON

By Henry Benbridge

mirably drawn, reserved in coloring, and dignified and natural in pose.

For his likeness of Washington, which could hardly compete with Gilbert Stuart's fine Vaughn portrait, painted at the same time, Peale went to considerable pains to win popular acclaim, advertising it as "the only true likeness" and obtaining numerous certificates attesting its merit. As he thereby incurred the odium of having inaugurated in this country the questionable practice of using certificates and the opinions of important persons to influence the public in accepting paintings, it is but fair to add that this unfortunate incident stands almost by itself in his life, and is in contradiction to his upright character as a gentleman and an artist.

Rembrandt Peale began drawing before he was ten years old, and at the age of thirteen devoted his time almost exclusively to art, painting a portrait of himself which was his second attempt from life. In 1796, Charles Willson Peale, giving up portraiture, recommended his son Rembrandt as his successor. The latter practised for several years in Charleston, South Carolina, and in 1801 went to England with his family, and studied under

Benjamin West. In 1807 and 1809 he visited Paris, painting the David and Houdon portraits already mentioned.

In 1810 he returned to the United States and worked in Baltimore, Philadelphia, New York, and Boston. In the spring of 1833 he was established in London, and practising there as a portrait-painter. He was one of the first artists in the United States to apply himself to lithography, and in 1827 was awarded a silver medal by the Franklin Institute of Philadelphia for one of his lithographs of Washington. He made in all thirty-nine copies in oils of his father's Washington portrait, and seventy-nine of his own, besides many copies of others by Stuart.

Washington Allston

Charles Fraser the miniaturist and Washington Allston are the two preëminent artists native to South Carolina. Both practised portraiture, and each with conspicuous success, though Allston devoted the greater part of his energies to the painting of historical and religious compositions, such as the "Christ Healing the Sick," "David Playing the Harp before Saul," and "The Massacre of the Innocents."

Born in the Waccammaw section of South Carolina in 1779, Allston on account of his health was sent when but seven years old to Newport, Rhode Island, then one of the most wealthy and cultivated communities in the country, to be educated. He could hardly have been sent to a place where his youthful enthusiasm for art would have received a greater impetus. As early as 1730, Newport boasted a private art gallery; it was closely associated with the work of John Smibert, and was the home of Edward Greene Malbone the miniaturist, later one of Allston's intimate friends.

As a boy, Allston made pictures in India ink and water-color, and in the days of his schooling had much incidental instruction in art from Samuel King, who made nautical instruments but had been trained as a painter and occasionally did portraits. Besides giving him instruction, King encouraged the young artist, and one of Allston's first oil paintings was a portrait of King, of which it is said that the head has a noble and striking contour, while the face is filled with a pleasing benignity.

From his school in Newport, young Allston went to Harvard College, and there continued to devote his leisure time to drawing, either of figures or of landscape. He also became acquainted for the first time with the Old Masters through Smibert's copies, and with the earlier American portraiture, much of which was produced in Boston and still remained in the immediate vicinity.

In 1803, together with John Vanderlyn, Allston went abroad, visited London and Paris and traveled leisurely through Switzerland to Italy, arriving in Rome in 1805—where, to use his own words, "It is needless to say how I was affected by Raphael."

Vanderlyn has described how he, Allston, Turner, and James Fenimore Cooper frequented a famous old café there. Cooper says that "there was something inexpressibly fascinating in his [Allston's] appearance and manners," and it is recorded that Allston exercised a sort of fascination upon all whom he met. Cooper wrote of him: "He was of a light and graceful form, with large blue eyes and black silken hair, waving and curling round a pale expressive countenance," and "was exquisitely sensitive to the graceful and beautiful, and took great delight in paintings which excelled in color."

Many of Allston's earlier works were portraits.

Property of Mrs. R. H. Baker, Norfolk, Virginia

PLATE XXVIII A

MRS. DANIEL CARY BARRAUD

Painted in 1770 by John Durand

Estate of Mrs. H. B. Mygatt, New Milford, Connecticut

PLATE XXVIII B

ITHAMAR CANFIELD

Painted in 1799 by Richard Jennys

He painted a self-portrait in 1805, and upon his return from Europe in 1809, devoting some of his time to portraiture, received higher prices than Gilbert Stuart, who charged one hundred dollars for a bust and a hundred and fifty for a twenty-eight by thirty-six inch canvas. His studio on Court Street in Boston, where Smibert had worked many years before, saw the completion of several likenesses of local celebrities. Benjamin West, whose portrait Allston also painted, told a friend that the latter "should never have left London. His course here was plain—his success certain." In 1811 he again went to London—this time with Samuel F. B. Morse, and from Morse we learn that "Allston was a severe teacher and an unflinching critic."

The artist himself ranked his likeness of Samuel Taylor Coleridge and that of Dr. King, both painted in England, among his best works. He also painted while there Robert Southey the poet. In 1819, after his return to Boston, he was made an associate of the Royal Academy, an honor which he did not fail to appreciate, for next to his native country he loved England.

By this time the delightful personality of the

artist, who in his younger days was so graceful in the dance that others paused to admire him, had considerably altered. Chester Harding, who came to be perhaps his most intimate friend, says that his habits were peculiar, that he lived alone, his studio a large old barn which was never swept. Nevertheless, he was universally recognized as the American "old master" of his day, and the greatest of our artists. George Inness had praised his work to the disadvantage of that of Gilbert Stuart and Sir Thomas Lawrence and virtually all of his fellow-painters looked upon him as a genius comparable to one of the giants of the Dutch seventeenth-century school or of the Italian renaissance.

John Wesley Jarvis

The nephew of John Wesley the famous Methodist preacher, John Wesley Jarvis, came to America with his parents in 1783 and settled first in Philadelphia. There as a boy he helped decorate fire-buckets and tradesmen's signs, made the friendship of Matthew Pratt, then an old man, and met Gilbert Stuart. From David Edwin the engraver he learned to draw and engrave. He later removed to New

New Milford Historical Society, New Milford, Connecticut

PLATE XXIX

MRS. SHERMAN BOARDMAN

Painted in 1796 by Ralph Earl

York, and was the best portrait-painter in that city for a number of years.

The quality of Jarvis's portraiture is attested by the fact that the fastidious Edward Greene Malbone visited his studio with some friends to see the pictures, and ended by instructing Jarvis in the art of portrait-painting in miniature. For a time his studio was on Broadway opposite the City Hall, and while there he was constantly occupied, painting portraits in oil, drawing profiles, and doing an occasional miniature on ivory when required. Later he worked successfully in Baltimore for more than a year and visited farther south—where, because of his hospitality and his wit, as well as on account of his talents as an artist, he was well received. About 1809 he was asking one hundred dollars for a head and one hundred and fifty for heads and hands. The next year he visited Charleston, South Carolina. In 1813 he was again painting in Baltimore.

About 1834, when he went to New Orleans, he was in the habit of receiving six sitters a day, each sitting occupying an hour. Henry Inman, who accompanied him to New Orleans, added the backgrounds and drapery in his portraits, under the artist's direction.

In this way Jarvis managed to finish six portraits each week, to earn more than six thousand dollars, and to return to New York with three thousand dollars.

Jarvis, like most portrait-painters of his day, copied portraits by Gilbert Stuart, but never really appreciated that artist's work. William Dunlap insinuates that Jarvis's inability to imitate Stuart's coloring had much to do with his lack of enthusiasm for Stuart's pictures.

Jarvis had a social nature, was a rare raconteur and wit, fond of good company and good food, and was consequently a great favorite wherever he happened to be. His dinners were famous in their day. His popularity had much to do with his success, but his portraiture is of conspicuous merit, and deserves more attention than it has received in recent years. Even the series of historical portraits in the City Hall in New York are, seemingly, well-nigh forgotten. His likeness of Alexander Anderson, the first American wood-engraver, is in the permanent collection of the Metropolitan Museum of Art in New York City.

SAMUEL L. WALDO AND WILLIAM JEWETT

As a student of art, Samuel L. Waldo made his living by painting signs for hatters, butchers, and other tradesmen; but with fifteen dollars received for a likeness made while he was still a very young man he began business as a professional portrait-painter. The encouragement of a gentleman in Litchfield, Connecticut, started him on a prosperous career in his native State, and later he worked successfully in Charleston, South Carolina. In 1806 he went to England and studied for a time with Benjamin West in London. Upon his return, in 1809, he took a studio in New York, where he became at once the leading, if not the best, portrait-painter of the day, and had as sitters several of the mayors of the city, as well as many other well-known local figures. Some of his canvases, such as the "Major-General Andrew Jackson," belonging to Mr. William A. Fisher of Detroit, are excellently conceived and brilliantly executed; they are fine in color and notable in characterization, drawing, and modeling of head and features.

In 1816, Waldo took into partnership his pupil William Jewett (1795–1874), and most of the portraits emanating from his studio thereafter are joint works, stamped "Waldo & Jewett," in which it is virtually impossible now to determine exactly which parts were painted by which artist. The characteristics of these likenesses are a highly finished surface, a tendency to "sweetness" in coloring and conventionality in pose. They are almost invariably painted on light wooden panels, measuring about twenty-five by thirty inches.

Waldo continued to paint in his own name after the inauguration of the partnership, but always signed the portraits so painted. They so nearly approximate the joint works that many of the latter, left unstamped by the stencil of the firm, are now mistakenly attributed to him. Nineteen of the Waldo & Jewett portraits were exhibited at the National Academy in New York, in which city the artists maintained their studio, between 1820 and 1827. The likenesses painted exclusively by Waldo after the partnership was formed, are very few—from a dozen to twenty perhaps. The finest of them are the portraits of Andrew Jackson, already mentioned, and

John Trumbull (1756–1843), at the Yale Art Gallery, the self-portrait at the Metropolitan Museum of Art in New York, and the portrait of General Alexander Macomb (1782–1841) at the New York City Hall. Of the Waldo & Jewett works the likeness of Judge David Sherman Boardman (1768–1864), owned by the Historical Society of New Milford, Connecticut, is by far the best.

The son of Sherman Boardman, Judge Boardman, was descended from Daniel Boardman, the first settled minister in New Milford, and Roger Sherman, signer of the Declaration of Independence, who came there from Massachusetts in 1743. Daniel Boardman was a prominent figure in Connecticut, and a Judge of the Superior Court of the State for many years. In the Waldo-Jewett likeness, painted when he was eighty-five, the head is finely drawn, the features well modeled, and the flesh tints very subtle in their simulation of the coloring of age. The clear brown eyes, snowy hair, and serenity of expression add measurably to the dignity and charm of the portrait.

Both Waldo and Jewett painted occasional landscapes, and the former did still life also. Jewett exhibited as early as 1817 an "Old Woman and Little Girl by Firelight" and a religious subject, "Paul and Silas Released from Prison." The opinion that he was primarily a landscape artist, and that therefore his share in the joint portraits is confined to the brushing-in of the backgrounds and perhaps painting some of the draperies, is entirely unjustified. In 1878, only seventeen years after Waldo's death, H. W. French, in his "Art and Artists of Connecticut," wrote that Jewett painted so thoroughly in Waldo's manner that only the most experienced could distinguish the work of one from that of the other in their joint productions. It is decidedly improbable that any one to-day, more than fifty years later, could identify the hand of either in one of these works.

After Waldo's death, Jewett seems never to have painted another portrait, though he survived his master and partner for a matter of thirteen years. Considering his abilities, as exemplified in the youthful likeness of Asher Durand from his hand, this is difficult to believe. He was quite as competent a portrait-painter as Waldo, and it would be only natural that upon the death of the senior partner he should succeed to something of the custom accorded to the firm. It would not be surprising to discover at any time a portrait or portraits by Jewett painted subsequent to Waldo's death.

Thomas Sully

Thomas Sully, an English boy, was brought to this country at the age of nine. He went to school in Charleston, South Carolina, with Charles Fraser, from whom he received instruction in the rudiments of portrait-painting. He is recorded as having said that Fraser's kindness, and the progress he made in consequence of it, determined the course of his life. He was later placed with a French miniaturist, M. Belzons, for a time, and still later studied with his elder brother, Laurence Sully, a miniaturist, in Richmond, Virginia. In 1801, Thomas accompanied his brother to Norfolk, where he saw some of the portraits of Henry Benbridge and determined to abandon water-color painting in miniature for portraiture in oils.

His first sitter for a likeness in oils was a Mr. William Ormsted. This likeness was a small picture painted in the manner of Benbridge. Later Sully met Benbridge, whom he idolized in the manner of youth, and the older man encouraged his efforts and instructed him by painting his portrait, and in the course of the work explaining his palette, its arrangement, and the application of the tints.

It was not, however, until 1806 that Sully really began, in New York City, his career as a portrait-painter in oils. There he encountered both J. W. Jarvis and John Trumbull, from whom he gained not a little in addition to the modest store of his knowledge of painting. A specimen of his work was submitted to Gilbert Stuart through the offices of a mutual friend, and Stuart told the young artist, "Keep what you have got, and get as much as you can," an ambiguous bit of advice with more of encouragement in it than at first appears.

Thomas Sully lived to a considerable age, and eventually occupied a commanding position in his profession in this country. The best of his likenesses are those of men. They are few in number, and to come upon one unexpectedly is generally a great surprise. The portraits of James Ross (1762–1847),

Thomas B. Clarke Collection

PLATE XXX A

JOHN PECK

By John Johnston

Thomas B. Clarke Collection

PLATE XXX B

MRS. PHŒBE FREEMAN

By Jacob Eichholtz

at the Pennsylvania Academy in Philadelphia, and that of Major Thomas Biddle (1790–1831), in the Thomas B. Clarke collection, the latter painted in 1813 and the former in 1814, are two of his finest works.

Sully's most famous picture is unquestionably the portrait of Queen Victoria, painted at Buckingham Palace in 1838, six weeks before her coronation. The original sketch for the head in this canvas is now in the permanent collection of the Metropolitan Museum of Art in New York. The artist had the sense to paint the little queen ascending the steps to her throne, in that way overcoming the disadvantage of her short figure in a composition in the grand manner. But his art had for almost a decade been declining. His best canvases, generally speaking, were painted from 1810 to 1820. The chief fault of his portraiture is its insistence upon mere prettiness, to the detriment of any recognizable indication of personality or character. This is so pronounced in his portraits of women as to suggest the "pretty girl" type of the present day, which is all too familiar through its constant utilization in illustration and advertising.

John Paradise

Born in New Jersey, of English parents, John Paradise first worked with his father as a saddler and later as a printer. As a youth he copied prints and drew faces from life, and at eighteen years of age he was painting portraits in oil. After studying in Philadelphia, he began in 1803 to practise portrait-painting professionally.

From 1810 on, Paradise worked in New York City, where, being of a deeply religious nature, he was chosen to paint the likenesses of numerous ministers, which were reproduced in the "Methodist Magazine." These portraits were of the conventional sizes for busts and half-lengths. His best works, however, were the occasional likenesses he painted in smaller size, such as that of Jonathan Jeue. Here the head is well drawn, the picture charming in color and straightforward and unassuming in its character.

John J. Audubon

Internationally known as a naturalist, for his beautiful and accurate colored pictures of birds and

Thomas B. Clarke Collection

PLATE XXXI

MRS. RICHARD YATES

Painted in 1793 by Gilbert Stuart

animals, John J. Audubon, born in the West Indies, and of French descent, received his first instruction in drawing from Jacques Louis David in France, which country he visited in the early years of the last century.

In reality a cosmopolitan rather than of any specific nationality, Audubon traveled extensively throughout his life in his pursuit of the study of natural history. In 1824 he came to New York City with letters to a number of prominent American artists of that time, and later in the same year went to Meadville, Pennsylvania, where he is known to have painted several portraits.

The painstaking fidelity with which Audubon pictured birds and animals is not a characteristic of his portraiture. His likenesses, however, have the appearance of being sufficiently truthful to have satisfied the expectations of his sitters. Specimens of his work in the field of portraiture are extremely scarce; it is doubtful, indeed, if he found opportunity to undertake many portraits, so considerable is the number of his nature studies.

James Frothingham

Like John Paradise, James Frothingham began his business career in the employ of his father, who was a manufacturer of chaises, and the youth's early interest in art found expression in coloring chaise bodies. His first likeness from life was a drawing in black and white, his second a self-portrait in India ink, and his first work in oil colors a portrait of his grandfather. The procedure he at first followed in portraiture was unique. Beginning with the forehead, he finished a face feature by feature. Eventually he learned—from a man who had had some instruction from Gilbert Stuart—how to use a palette, arrange the colors thereon, and mix tints and use them.

At the age of twenty Frothingham abandoned the coloring of chaise bodies, and began to practise portrait-painting professionally. Finally he met Stuart, and that master, after at first discouraging him, gave him a number of lessons. In 1810, looking at a picture from Frothingham's brush, Stuart told the young artist, "There is no man in Boston, but myself, can paint so good a head." Soon afterward

Stuart said of another of Frothingham's portraits, "Except myself, there is no man in the United States can paint a better head than that."

Frothingham practised his profession in Charlestown, Salem, and Boston, Massachusetts, and in New York City. His portraits from 1810 on were, with the exception of Stuart's, the finest painted in this country, and the best of them can hang without disadvantage beside fine canvases by that master. In Frothingham's faces one finds more of the animation of a living presence, more of the character of a sitter revealed in his or her expression, than in any but the exceptional portraits of the greatest artists. His fidelity to nature compasses a sensitive transposition of feeling and emotion that is almost unique in portraiture. A likeness from his hand achieves at times almost the effect of a living presence, so perfectly does he invest it with the semblance of life. Technically, his command of his medium is as noteworthy as the charm and refinement of his color.

The present lack of interest in James Frothingham's work, and of enthusiasm for its undeniable quality, is to be explained only by the scarcity of good examples in public collections, and the consequent ignorance of its merit. His portraits of Mr. and Mrs. Jonathan Brooks, painted in 1823, now in the Art Museum of Worcester, Massachusetts, rank with the finest works in the field of portraiture produced in this country.

Matthew Harris Jouett

As a mere child Matthew Harris Jouett, born in Mercer County, Kentucky, was enough of an artist to impress his family and their neighbors with his skill in sketching from nature and making likenesses from life. His father, Captain John Jouett, was a farmer, so Matthew's boyhood was spent at farm labor. Finally Captain Jouett, who could not afford to give all his sons the advantages of an academic education, determined, in his manner of speaking, "to make a gentlemen of one," at least, and left to them the decision which it should be. Their choice was Matthew, the young artist, who therefore at seventeen entered Transylvania University, where he studied law. But his interest in art was not forgotten, and in such leisure as he found in the intervals of study he painted miniatures, delighting especially in making likenesses of women.

Wadsworth Athenæum, Hartford, Connecticut

PLATE XXXII

OZIAS HUMPHREY

By Gilbert Stuart

After a brief period of active service in the War of 1812, Jouett abandoned law and took up professionally the practice of portrait-painting, in Louisville, Kentucky, where for a time he barely managed to earn a living with his brush. A little later, receiving twenty-five dollars each for life-size canvases, and being a very rapid painter, he was doing three likenesses a week and making what then amounted to a comfortable income. In 1817, journeying on horseback to Philadelphia to see Benjamin West (who had, however, left for England before Jouett arrived), he met Gilbert Stuart, who became his teacher and incidentally painted his portrait.

Jouett returned to Kentucky, opened a studio in Lexington, and practised there successfully, though he had doubled his prices for portraits. In the winter he worked in New Orleans, and, his reputation extending to neighboring Southern cities, he was constantly employed, returning year after year, almost to the time of his death, to fill the orders he received. In 1824 he painted in Lexington his small full-length of La Fayette, and from that work the full-length in life-size which was purchased by the State and to-day hangs in the State House, or Capitol.

The artist was a handsome man, his features of an Irish cast, with dark-brown hair, gray-blue eyes, and a ruddy complexion. Tall and spare, he was well proportioned, and, owing somewhat to his military training, he was an impressive, almost aristocratic, figure. Brilliant as a conversationist, witty and quick at repartee, he was gentle and notably refined. When he was working upon a picture it absorbed his entire attention, and he was very impatient of any interruption.

Jouett's heads are well modeled, his coloring reserved and applied with a full brush and a free hand, even his miniatures being painted in the broad manner of oil painting, without stippling or hatching. He had a pronounced objection to bothering with the detail of dress, and the latter is summarily treated in most of his portraits, the head being emphasized as the thing of importance. Backgrounds he did very simply, with sufficient indication of atmosphere, however, to relieve the head and balance the warm and cool tones. Mobility of expression, the momentary look upon a face, he could not capture in a likeness as James Frothingham did, and

Cleveland Museum of Art, Cleveland, Ohio

PLATE XXXIII

GENERAL GEORGE WASHINGTON

Painted in 1783 by Joseph Wright

for this reason some of his likenesses fail to give entire satisfaction. He was the foremost early portrait-painter of the Middle West, and his works in both oil and miniature are of such merit as to deserve the serious attention of all who study early American portraiture.

Samuel F. B. Morse

After devoting the earlier years of his life to art, painting a number of very creditable portraits, among which the smaller sketch-like panels executed between 1815 and 1820 are worthy of special attention, Samuel F. B. Morse spent the remainder of his life perfecting the telegraph, which he invented in 1838. His first likenesses, painted while he was a student at Yale College, were miniatures on ivory, for which he charged five dollars each, the sitter supplying the ivory. After his graduation he studied for a few months with Washington Allston, and when but nineteen years old went to London, with letters to Benjamin West and John Singleton Copley. There he was much of a favorite with such men as the artists Turner and Sir Thomas Lawrence and the poets Coleridge and Wordsworth, who were charmed with his frank, warm-hearted youthful enthusiasm.

While he was studying with West, that master influenced his development as a painter materially, and his first works were in the field of historical composition. In this field he was fortunate enough to succeed to the extent of winning a medal from the Society of Arts in London for his picture "The Dying Hercules."

In 1815, Morse returned to Boston with his "Judgment of Jupiter," only to find that there was no demand for such works here. He therefore proceeded to New Hampshire, where he painted a number of cabinet portraits at fifteen dollars each. Hearing that he could get twice as much for them in Charleston, South Carolina, he went there and was immediately successful. Indeed, so fast did commissions follow one another that he painted an average of four cabinet portraits a week, and produced before he left in the summer of 1818 about one hundred and fifty.

The full-length life-size likeness of La Fayette which Morse painted in 1825 for the Corporation of the City of New York, and which now hangs in the City Hall, is one of the most impressive works of its kind ever produced in this country. The head is finely modeled, almost sculpturesque in effect, and the color scheme, while charming, is altogether dignified and in keeping with the character of the composition.

Standing upon an open portico with a mosaic flooring, against a stormy sky of dark clouds tinged with streaks of red, La Fayette appears in yellowish tan trousers, white waistcoat, shirt, collar, and tie, and a black or very dark-blue coat with a cape of the same color, the red lining of which shows at his left shoulder. His right hand rests lightly on a parapet at the left, on which are sculptured busts of Washington and Franklin. A more impressive arrangement would be difficult to contrive.

The head of Mayor William Paulding, also at the City Hall in New York, has the same sculpturesque quality, the modeling being expressive in a sense rarely achieved in painting.

An example of Morse's early work in cabinet size, the "Rev. and Mrs. Hiram Bingham," painted in Boston in 1819, may be seen at the Yale Art Gallery. Seeing it gives one something of the thrill of discovering a rare and beautiful type of portrait. It has the freedom of touch and immediacy of a sketch, and the finality of a finished interpretation of individual character. The Rev. Hiram Bingham was one of several missionaries who, accompanied by their wives, sailed from Boston in 1819 for stations in the Pacific islands. Morse painted small double portraits of them all. Another of them, now owned by a descendant in New Milford, Connecticut, is quite as effective, being charmingly posed and ingratiatingly intimate in its human appeal. Generally his larger, more formal likenesses of women lack interest because of an undue emphasis on colorful costume and elaborate coiffure.

Morse settled in New York City in 1825, and was one of the founders and the first president of the National Academy of Design. After five years under Washington Allston and Benjamin West, he was for twenty-three years a professional portrait-painter, and in that period produced a creditable number of likenesses of first-rate importance, notwithstanding the fact that he was neither a great technician nor a great colorist. Within his limitations, however, he probably reached as high a degree of excellence in portraiture as was possible. When, as a student in London, he submitted a carefully finished drawing to West time after time only to be told to "go on and finish it," and, finally, that "it is not numerous drawings, but the character of one, which makes a thorough draftsman," he learned a valuable lesson—and profited by it in after years. As a draftsman, he ranks with the best of our portrait-painters.

Chester Harding

After trying to earn a living, first as a chair-maker in Massachusetts, where he was born, and later as a tavern-keeper in western New York, Chester Harding, with his family, went to Pittsburgh, Pennsylvania. There he conceived the idea of becoming a portrait-painter, and he had his likeness and his wife's painted by an ornamental sign- and portrait-painter, in the hope of learning something of advantage to himself. His first canvas, a portrait of his wife, was successful enough to encourage him to remove to Paris, Kentucky (a frontier town in those days), and open a studio, charging twenty-five dollars for his canvases. After painting about a hundred portraits there, he went to Philadelphia to study the work of Thomas Sully, returning at the end of a few weeks, disconcerted at the comparison of his own work with that of Sully and other artists.

Harding moved from Kentucky, tried his fortune in several cities, and eventually settled in St. Louis, where he practised successfully until July, 1821, charging forty dollars for his likenesses. Late in 1821 he went to Washington, D. C., where he exhibited a few heads and painted forty or fifty canvases during the winter and early spring. The following autumn he spent a week in Boston, practised for a time in Northampton, Massachusetts, and finally returned to work in Boston. He painted something like eighty portraits in the course of six months, having more sitters than Gilbert Stuart himself. He was sensible enough to understand, however, that his portraits could not be compared with Stuart's in any way, and modestly attributed his own popularity to an unusual interest in himself as a self-taught painter.

In 1823, Harding went to London, where he painted a number of canvases and exhibited at the Royal Academy. That he must have enjoyed a considerable popularity and lived well in London is demonstrated by the fact that the twelve thousand dollars which he earned in three years there was just sufficient to cover his expenses. Before returning to the United States he paid a short visit to Paris, and reached Boston in the autumn of 1826.

Self-taught as he was, Harding managed in exceptional instances to paint some really first-rate portraits, such as the "Loammi Baldwin." Most of his likenesses, however, are of the conventional sort that never rises much above mediocrity. William Dunlap wrote of him in 1834 as "standing in the foremost rank of portrait-painters in the United States"—a much exaggerated opinion, probably based upon Harding's popularity at the time and a personal liking for him as a man, because of his modesty and sincerity.

James Barton Longacre

Better known as an engraver than as a portrait-painter, James Barton Longacre, born in Pennsylvania, studied engraving in Philadelphia with George Murray, and portraiture in oil probably with some other artist in that city. Together with James Herring, he conceived the idea of "The American

Portrait Gallery," consisting of biographical sketches and likenesses of military and naval heroes, statesmen, and authors. Many of the originals of the engraved portraits in the three volumes of this work were cabinet-size oils from Longacre's hand. They are of sufficient merit to warrant our including him among the American portrait-painters of the end of the eighteenth century.

Lucius Munson

Lucius Munson as a very young man was encouraged by a friend who was an artist to give up farming as a means of earning a livelihood and to follow his natural inclination toward painting. He began as a professional portrait-painter in New Haven, Connecticut, in 1815, and worked in New York City in 1817 and 1818. In 1820 he practised for a while in South Carolina, and the next year went to Bermuda, with the intention of going on to Europe as soon as his means would permit. He died on Turk's Island in 1822, when only twenty-six years of age. His self-portrait at the New Haven Colony Historical Society, even in its present miserable physical condition, shows him to have been an artist of un-

Property of Mr. George Dudley Seymour

PLATE XXXIV A

LAURA WELLS CHURCHILL

Painted about 1814 by Samuel Broadbent

Thomas B. Clarke Collection

PLATE XXXIV B

HENRY ECKFORD

Painted in 1809 by Robert Fulton

usual talent and great promise, who probably would have risen to eminence in his profession had he lived even to middle age.

John Neagle

After an apprenticeship with a coach-painter who had more than a little to do with arousing his ambition to become an artist, John Neagle, who had received a few lessons from Bass Otis, a second-rate portrait-painter, began to paint likenesses professionally when but twenty years old. His attempts at portraiture while still an apprentice had been encouraged by Charles Willson Peale, Thomas Sully, and other artists, from which fact it may reasonably be inferred that his works had real merit of one kind or another. He was particularly successful in getting a good likeness—so much so that in later years, when an established artist, he said that, however he had improved otherwise, he could not have improved upon the *likeness* as realized in his first portraits.

After a futile attempt to find a place for himself as a portrait-painter in Kentucky and Louisiana, he returned to Philadelphia (where he had worked as a youth), married a daughter of Thomas Sully, and became very successful. His painting continued to improve, and in 1826 his full-length life-size figure of the wealthy blacksmith Pat Lyon, a carte-blanche commission, excited wide attention and well-deserved praise. By permission he painted a duplicate of it for the Boston Athenæum. The original canvas, after being exhibited in Philadelphia, was shown at the National Academy of Design in New York City, where it was the foremost artistic success of the day. In its particular genre, no finer picture has ever been painted in this country.

Gilbert Stuart, whose likeness Neagle painted, treated him well, and Washington Allston, who also was a friend of his, complimented him on the likeness. In his finer canvases, such as the portraits of Gilbert Stuart and Richard M. Johnson (1781–1850), he challenges comparison with the best artists of his time. He had a happy faculty for securing an effectual pose, which contributed much to the success of his work, but the chief merit of his portraits is that they are lifelike and accurate. He practised none of the trickery of technic in obtaining his effects, and his method and color conform pretty generally to the established custom of the day.

PLATE XXXV

SELF-PORTRAIT

By Mather Brown

Nathaniel Jocelyn

One of the large band of Connecticut copper-plate engravers, Nathaniel Jocelyn, in early life did portraits in miniature, in pencil, and, later, in oil. For a time, in 1820, he practised in Savannah, Georgia. In the years following 1826, when he first exhibited at the National Academy in New York City, he attained an enviable position as a portrait-painter. From 1826 to 1831 he showed altogether ten canvases at the Academy, but his name does not appear as that of an exhibitor thereafter, and he probably decided to make his home in New Haven and work there exclusively.

Enough of an artist in his own right to realize his limitations, Jocelyn recognized the obvious superiority of other painters exhibiting at the Academy, and wisely chose to escape the competition he could not meet, by removing to his native city where his talents were appreciated. There his townsmen and the faculty of Yale College supplied him with commissions sufficient to keep him busy and afford him a comfortable living. He returned to New Haven with honors, for he had been made a member of the National Academy in 1828, and this was enough evidence of the esteem in which his art was held in the metropolis to impress favorably the people of New Haven.

While his technic lacks something of the finish of that of Samuel Waldo and William Jewett, and though he sometimes fails lamentably in drawing, his heads are almost invariably well modeled and solidly painted, and probably his likenesses were in the main really successful. His coloring falls within a limited range, and in the lower register save in exceptional cases. He painted many of the Yale faculty, and most of his remaining likenesses are of men. The finest of his works, at the Yale Art Gallery, include the "Eli Ives," the "William Leffingwell," and the "Mrs. Augustus Street," the last-named one of his rare female portraits, especially notable for its variety of color and as a spirited presentation of vivacious youthful personality.

It can hardly be contended that Jocelyn belongs in the first rank of our portrait-painters, but he stands well in the forefront of those of the second class.

Asher B. Durand

The art life of Asher Durand may be divided into three well-defined periods. The first, from 1812 to 1832, was devoted to engraving; the second, from 1833 to 1838, to portraiture; and the third, from 1839 onward, to landscape—chiefly studies of trees. Probably the greatest of our engravers, in portrait-painting he found his facility as an engraver of little or no assistance. He visualized a sitter as form in which detail was of virtually no consequence. His method was therefore altered to meet other conditions than those imposed by the painstaking rendering of detail, and in the unaccustomed freedom of a different manner of expression he managed to achieve only a modest success.

Between 1822, when he painted the portrait of his mother, and the eighteen-thirties, Durand produced, however, a number of really interesting portraits. The "Luman Reed" owned by the New York Historical Society, painted with a measure of freedom and accuracy of touch, and reserved in color, represents him at his best. While acceptable as likenesses, his portraits seldom attain distinction. His coloring, though right in its place, fails to give life to his sitters. His technic is too constrained, his touch too careful, ever to permit of that freedom which is the basic necessity of great art. Unable to originate a method adapted to his individual requirements, he worked in the customary manner of the time.

The early portrait of Durand's mother is intriguing; it is more of a sketch than a finished painting, and yet somehow curiously impressive in its unassuming sincerity. The self-portrait, on the other hand, a more finished figure, is too obviously posed for effect to be really successful in a vital sense as a likeness.

Yale Art Gallery, New Haven, Connecticut

PLATE XXXVI

GEORGE WASHINGTON

Painted in 1792 by John Trumbull

PART III

PORTRAIT-PAINTERS OF THE EARLY NINETEENTH CENTURY

LIST OF PAINTERS

Francis Alexander	American	1800–1880
Henry Inman	American	1801–1846
William J. Hubard	English	1807–1862
James Reed Lambdin	American	1807–1889
George W. Twibill	American	1808–1836
Oliver Frazer	American	1808–1864
Charles Loring Elliott	American	1812–1868
William S. Jewett	American	1812–1873
Emanuel Leutze	German	1816–1869
George W. Flagg	American	1816–1897
Daniel Huntington	American	1816–1906

Museum of Fine Arts, Boston, Massachusetts

PLATE XXXVII

MRS. STEPHEN MINOTT

By John Trumbull

PART III

PORTRAIT-PAINTERS OF THE EARLY NINETEENTH CENTURY

FRANCIS ALEXANDER

A RESIDENT of Connecticut, born in 1800, Francis Alexander first studied art with Alexander Robinson the miniaturist, and probably his earliest portraits were miniatures painted in water-color on ivory. In his twenties he went to Boston, with a letter from John Trumbull to Gilbert Stuart, and studied with the latter, advancing rapidly in his painting under Stuart's influence. Besides several likenesses of Daniel Webster, he painted one of Charles Dickens, one of Benjamin R. Curtis, and many others. Some of his finest canvases are of women, whom he painted most successfully, with a fine realization of their personal character in his likenesses.

Francis Alexander and William S. Jewett, dealt with hereafter, are the two best American portrait-painters of the first half of the nineteenth century.

Henry Inman

Henry Inman was born in Utica, New York, in 1801, and went with his parents to New York City in 1812. There he received his first regular instruction in drawing. His father encouraged the boy's interest in art, and used to take him to exhibitions. In 1814 he became the pupil of John Wesley Jarvis, at that artist's request. With his instructor he visited New Orleans and other cities. After several years of study with Jarvis, he began painting portraits in oil and miniatures in New York.

William Dunlap's statement that Inman's work in miniature is second only to that of E. G. Malbone is the most flagrant sort of exaggeration. Inman's ivories are not to be compared with either Charles Fraser's or James Peale's. His pupil in miniature-painting, Thomas S. Cummings, was about the poorest practitioner of his day.

Inman's likenesses in oil are what really entitle him to some attention, at least, as a portrait-painter. While they offer nothing individual in style or technic, in the mode of the period they compare favorably with anything of American production with which they had to compete. In pose they are generally academic in character, but the heads are well modeled and the expression in the faces especially well rendered.

William J. Hubard

An English prodigy in the art of silhouette-cutting, William J. Hubard came to this country when a mere boy and for some years practised that art, being popularly known as "Master Hubard." Robert W. Weir the painter first encouraged him to try portrait-painting in oil, and he had some assistance from Thomas Sully. Although his oil portraits are much less attractive than his silhouettes (the latter being of the best of that type of thing), he managed to exhibit at the National Academy in the eighteen-thirties. A likeness of John C. Calhoun from his easel may be seen at the Corcoran Art Gallery in Washington, D. C. Probably his best works, however, are the "Charles Carroll," owned by the Maryland Historical Society, and the "Henry Clay."

James Reed Lambdin

West of the Alleghanies, James Reed Lambdin was the best portrait-painter in the second quarter of the nineteenth century. He received instruction in Philadelphia from Edward Miles and Thomas Sully in the early eighteen-twenties. Later he settled in Louisville, Kentucky, and there practised successfully for a number of years, then returned, in 1838, to Philadelphia. There and in Washington he painted portraits for the rest of his life. His sitters included several of the Presidents, Chief Justice Marshall, Daniel Webster, and Henry Clay.

George W. Twibill

A native of Pennsylvania, George Twibill went as a youth to New York City, where he studied first with an artist named Parissien. Later he was a pupil of the National Academy and of Henry Inman, who was his brother-in-law. He won something of a reputation as a painter of oil portraits "in little," which he began to paint professionally in 1832.

The most characteristic and truthful likeness we have of John Trumbull the artist, as he appeared in his old age, is said to be Twibill's full-length, cabinet-size portrait, painted in 1835.

Owing to George Twibill's early death these little

Museum of Fine Arts, Boston, Massachusetts

PLATE XXXVIII

MR. STEPHEN MINOTT

By John Trumbull

likenesses of his are extremely rare—indeed, almost unknown to us to-day.

Oliver Frazer

After studying with Matthew Harris Jouett in Kentucky, where he was born, Oliver Frazer, at Jouett's suggestion, continued his studies with Thomas Sully in Philadelphia. In 1834 he went abroad, and studied in Paris under the same master as George P. A. Healy, an American portrait-painter of a later day. Upon his return he proceeded to Lexington, Kentucky, opened a studio, and began professionally the practice of portrait-painting. In appearance well proportioned, slightly over medium height, graceful in movement and dignified in manner, he soon atttracted friends and patrons, and as early as 1837 was receiving fifty dollars for a head—the highest price charged by established artists in Kentucky at that time.

Frazer's likenesses are uneven in quality, and many of them lack human interest such as comes from incisive characterization. His best portraits are those of men. Women, in his opinion, too generally wished to be made to appear pretty, regardless of whether they were so or not, and he seems to have painted them mostly without sufficient enthusiasm to admit of success. In drawing and in pose, his figures are adequate but unimpressive. His faces are more satisfying, well modeled, and in many instances not without definitely indicated expression. His technic is that of his time, without those peculiarities of a personal nature which are invariably the hall-mark of originality in painting. Within the limitations of its type his portraiture, however, escapes being merely commonplace; and the best of his likenesses, such as the "Henry Clay," might hang without discredit beside others of their time.

Charles Loring Elliott

Born in the village of Scipio, New York, Charles Loring Elliott went to New York City in the eighteen-thirties, and studied with John Trumbull. In 1846 he was made a member of the National Academy, but long before that he was practising professionally as a portrait-painter. More facile than his master, and more finished in his style, he had literally hundreds of sitters. His portraiture,

Metropolitan Museum of Art, New York City

Plate XXXIX

GEORGE WASHINGTON

Painted in 1795 by Adolph Ulrich Wertmuller

however, is entirely of the academic type, undistinguished by any evidence of individual and illuminating characteristics in the way of technic, composition, pose, or coloring. His portrait of Asher B. Durand is in the permanent collection of the Corcoran Art Gallery in Washington.

William S. Jewett

William S. Jewett, who in 1838 won the first prize, a gold palette, in a students' competition at the National Academy, seems to have retired on his laurels at that time, contenting himself with painting likenesses of his family only. Though he is not widely known, his portraits are the equal of any painted in the United States in their day; they are subdued yet attractive in color, and the faces glow with life. That of his sister, painted in 1842, and another of a distant relative, William Forest, painted in 1846, are privately owned in Kent, Connecticut. The Forest portrait is an especially interesting work, and as fine an example of "a speaking likeness" as one will find in the art of its day.

Jewett went to California with the "forty-niners,"

and there painted professionally so successfully as to be able to put aside funds sufficient for an investment that eventually made him wealthy for those times. In all probability many examples of his portraiture are still preserved in California by descendants of the miners for whom he painted them. He must not be confused with the William Jewett mentioned in an earlier chapter, who painted with Samuel L. Waldo, under the signature of "Waldo & Jewett."

Emanuel Leutze

Brought to America while still but a child, Emanuel Leutze grew up in Philadelphia, where his parents settled, studied with John A. Smith, a portrait-painter in that city, and later in Düsseldorf, Germany. His earliest works were in the field of portraiture, and he painted at one time, for purposes of engraving, heads of many of the leading American statesmen at Washington, D. C. In 1850 he received a gold medal in Berlin for his large historical composition, "Washington Crossing the Delaware," a replica of which is at the Metropolitan Museum of Art in New York City.

But notwithstanding his consequent popularity as a historical painter, he continued to paint likenesses, some of which are singularly attractive, admirable in technic, fine in color, and surprising in the degree to which they simulate the effect of a living presence. These later portraits are often of generous size, half- or three-quarter length, and generally both signed and dated. Probably his most famous sitter was General Grant, whose portrait dates from Civil War times.

George W. Flagg

George W. Flagg, a versatile artist born in New Haven, Connecticut, spent his boyhood in Charleston, South Carolina, and much of his youth abroad. About 1830 he settled in Boston and began the practice of portrait-painting, though his works include, as well, religious and historical compositions and pictures from dramatic and literary sources. His likeness of Washington Allston, who was his uncle, is probably as fine as any American portrait of its date, admirable in its revelation of character and in the simple dignity of its composition and coloring.

Daniel Huntington

Daniel Huntington, born in New York, first felt an inclination to pursue the practice of art in John Trumbull's studio, but Trumbull assured him that it was a precarious vocation. However, it seems that later acquaintance with an itinerant portrait-painter, while Huntington was a student at Hamilton College, decided the matter. At about this time the young man sat to Charles Loring Elliott, and while doing so made use of Elliott's brushes and palette to try his own hand at likenesses of some of his classmates.

In 1835, Huntington began the study of painting with Samuel F. B. Morse, and later he studied with Henry Inman. His earliest works were humorous subjects from everyday life, but he was already painting portraits professionally before 1836. His likenesses of Gulian C. Verplanck, Morse (his master), Chancellor James Kent, and Dr. Muhlenberg of New York are numbered among his early portraits. Four portraits from his hand may be seen at the Metropolitan Museum of Art in New York City.

PART IV

MINIATURE-PAINTERS OF THE EIGHTEENTH AND EARLY NINETEENTH CENTURIES

LIST OF PAINTERS

John Ramage	Irish	1802
Walter Robertson	Irish	1820
Matthew Pratt	American	1734–1805
John Singleton Copley	American	1738–1815
Charles Willson Peale	American	1741–1827
Henry Pelham	American	1749 ?1806
James Peale	American	1749–1831
William Verstille	American	1755–1803
John Trumbull	American	1756–1843
Joseph Dunkerley	English	Working 1785
Edward Savage	American	1761–1817
Robert Fulton	American	1765–1815
Archibald Robertson	Scotch	1765–1835
Benjamin Trott	American	Working 1790–1833
William Dunlap	American	1766–1839
Edward Greene Malbone	American	1777–1807
Rembrandt Peale	American	1778–1860
John Wesley Jarvis	English	1780–1839
Elkanah Tisdale	American	Working early 1800's
Anson Dickinson	American	1780–1852
Charles Fraser	American	1782–1860
Thomas Sully	English	1783–1872
Matthew Harris Jouett	American	1787–1827

LIST OF PAINTERS (*Continued*)

Nathaniel Rogers	American	1788–1844
Samuel F. B. Morse	American	1791–1872
Anna Claypoole Peale	American	1791–1878
Robert Field	English	1819
George Catlin	American	1796–1872
Thomas Sier Cummings	American	1804–1894
Henry Colton Shumway	American	1807–1884

New York ***Public Library***

PLATE XL A

GEORGE WASHINGTON

By James Peale

Ehrich Galleries, New York City

PLATE XL B

HENRY CLAY

By James Reed Lambdin

PART IV

MINIATURE-PAINTERS OF THE EIGHTEENTH AND EARLY NINETEENTH CENTURIES

THERE are many types of miniatures, but for the sake of lucidity only those painted in water-color on ivory are designated herein as "true" miniatures. Besides these are others in water-color on porcelain and paper, in oil on ivory and wood, and in either medium on metal. The technic is almost as varied as the types of miniatures, including stippling, hatching, wash, and the customary brushing in oil. In size, these little portraits average about two and a half or three inches in height and two or two and a half inches in width.

In the course of a hundred years miniature art reached in America a limit of excellence unsurpassed by any foreign practitioners, with the possible exception of Holbein. Neither Cosway nor Englehart in England, nor Isaby in France, excelled Edward Greene Malbone, Charles Fraser, James Peale, John

Singleton Copley, and Henry Pelham, who were all native-born artists and painted virtually all their ivories in this country. John Ramage and Walter Robertson, two Irishmen who settled in America in the last third of the eighteenth century, and Robert Field, an Englishman who practised here from 1795 to 1806, were veritable masters of this "portraiture in little."

From 1776 until early in the nineteenth century, miniatures enjoyed a great popularity with the wealthy and cultured in all parts of the country, and were commissioned in considerable numbers in all the larger cities along the Atlantic coast, from Boston to Savannah. Malbone practised professionally in Boston, Newport, Providence, New York, Charleston, and Savannah, but generally speaking, our miniaturists confined their labors to some one well-defined locality: Copley and Henry Pelham to Boston, Ramage to New York, James Peale to Philadelphia, Robert Field to Washington and Maryland, and Fraser to Charleston.

The first of our important native practitioners, in order of birth, are Matthew Pratt, John Singleton Copley, and Charles Willson Peale; the greatest in

City Hall, New York City

PLATE XLI

MARQUIS DE LA FAYETTE

Painted in 1824 by Samuel F. B. Morse

their achievement are Malbone and Fraser; and probably the last, at least of those whose works were uninfluenced by photography, is Henry Colton Shumway, who after the Civil War was reduced to the necessity of tinting photographs, so thoroughly had the photographer replaced the miniaturist. From 1830 to 1860, Shumway's ivories were conspicuously popular with the public, and during that period he was the reigning master of miniature-painting in New York City.

JOHN RAMAGE

A typical Irishman, with English sympathies, John Ramage came to America and settled in Boston just before the outbreak of the Revolution. He married, deserted his wife, and sailed to Canada with Lord Howe in 1776, probably to escape criticism and perhaps active service in the conflict. Later he went to New York, with another wife, became a respected citizen of that city, moved in the best society, and was notably successful in the practice of his profession. He painted George Washington for the general's wife, besides miniatures of the Ludlows, Van Cortlandts, Pintards, General Anthony Wayne,

General Alexander McDougall, and many other prominent figures of the day. Being a goldsmith as well as a painter, he made the handsome little lockets in which most of his ivories were set.

His finer portraits compare favorably with any of their time, but he was uneven in his work, and when his hand was unsteady through indulgence in drink his miniatures were correspondingly inartistic in every sense—hard and dry in color, and stiff and formal in their rendering of the sitter. Nevertheless, in the seventeen-eighties he was the best miniaturist working in New York and was very successful, painting most of the great landowners and merchants, military and civil officers, and belles and beaux of the city. He was fashionable in his dress, gay and witty in his conversation, and naturally enjoyed a considerable popularity. Ivories from his hand may be seen at the Metropolitan Museum of Art and the New York Historical Society in New York City.

Walter Robertson

Walter Robertson appeared in New York City in the early seventeen-nineties. Like John Ramage, he was Irish and a painter of miniatures, but his work was decidedly superior to Ramage's. He evidently fell heir to the popularity of Ramage when the latter left this country and went to Canada, and for several years he practised with conspicuous success. Among his sitters were Martha Washington and Lawrence Reid Yates, the latter a prosperous and well-known merchant of New York.

His ivories average about two and a half inches high by two inches in width, and are painted with meticulous care. The heads are well modeled, the features faithfully drawn, and the faces, though somewhat lacking in expression, nevertheless achieve a sense of living reality. His tints are pure, and in values sensitively modulated to conform to the scheme of color in almost every instance. While none of his works reach the perfection of John Singleton Copley's diminutive ivories in exquisite passages of fastidiously manipulated hues in the higher register, he manages to impress one very favorably as a colorist in the less difficult practice of a more customary range of hues.

Robertson arrived in this country in 1793, on the ship that brought Gilbert Stuart, whom he had known in London and many of whose portraits he is reputed to have copied in miniature. His style is remarkable for purity of color and precision of drawing, resulting in a highly artistic product, almost on a par with that of Edward Greene Malbone. His flesh tints are good, the features accurately though sensitively drawn, and the eyes alight with life. The likenesses of George and Martha Washington are among the best we have of that couple; the former work was adopted by other artists as a model, and the latter is unsurpassed even by Charles Fraser's ivories of elderly women, which are particularly fine.

Robertson must have enjoyed a considerable popularity in the few years he remained in the United States, and probably painted as many as thirty or forty miniatures, eleven of which were shown at the Metropolitan Museum exhibition of American Miniatures in New York City in 1927. Two of his ivories may be seen in the permanent collection of that institution.

Matthew Pratt

Though Matthew Pratt has already been recorded as a painter of miniatures, it is only now,

Yale Art Gallery, New Haven, Connecticut

PLATE XLII

MRS. AUGUSTUS RUSSELL STREET

By Nathaniel Jocelyn

for the first time, that an actual ivory from his hand can be described. Painted about 1775, it pictures at half-length, standing, Mildred and Catharine, two of the daughters of Warner and Hannah Washington of Fairfax, Virginia, who had in all seven children.

Mildred, born in 1765, and Catharine, in 1767, appear as children of ten and eight, each with an arm about the other. The pose is stiff, the technic is competent but without individuality; and the miniature, while naïve, is hardly attractive. It is, however, interesting as preserving the likenesses of two of George Washington's relatives, and on account of its being the only authenticated work of the kind by Pratt, whose hitherto recorded works number but nineteen, including those attributed to him as well as those he is known to have painted.

This particular ivory is circular, three and three eighths inches in diameter, and is signed at the right "M. Pratt." Though Pratt was a master of portraiture in oil, this example proves him to have been anything but successful as a miniaturist.

John Singleton Copley

From 1755 to 1769, in the very beginning of his career as an artist and when he was a mere youth, John Singleton Copley painted, in the vicinity of Boston, perhaps as many as twenty true miniatures, diminutive in size and unique in their delicacy of coloring in the lighter hues. Even the characteristic emphasis of outline and the mask-like fixity of his faces is greatly modified by this intriguing chromatic scheme, which makes them doubly precious when in anything like their original state. Unfortunately, his delicate tints were notoriously evanescent, and have all but disappeared from some of his most important ivories, particularly the "Washington" of 1755, which may be seen at the Metropolitan Museum of Art in New York.

On the other hand, the "Mr. and Mrs. Samuel Cary" at the Art Museum of Worcester, Massachusetts, the self-portrait on loan at the Boston Museum of Fine Arts, and the "Penelope Dwelly" (Mrs. John Aspinwall), painted about 1758, which is in a private collection in New York, all preserve

New York Historical Society, New York City

PLATE XLIII

LUMAN REED

By Asher B. Durand

the pristine delicacy of his original exquisite coloring.

Several of the latest examples that have come to light, such as the "Thomas Kast" of 1769, at the New Haven Colony Historical Society, and the "Barnabas Deane," are but the ghosts of their former selves, little more than the skeleton or outline of the likeness remaining.

Copley, who achieved a considerable reputation as a portrait-painter in oil early in life, evidently discontinued working in miniature before he left America in 1774, and even before that he was not a regular practitioner of miniature-painting. His ivories resemble his oils in arrangement, and somewhat in technic as well, though he used both stippling and hatching at times. Green and blue in modified values are characteristic of his miniatures. His coloring is invariably cool, and generally darker in the female and lighter in the male portraits. In size they average approximately one and a quarter by one inch, several being even smaller. Almost all were set in plain gold lockets, some of which had a pin at the back to permit of their use as brooches. Their remarkable perfection as works of art, considering their compass, is conspicuous, and has never been approached by any other artist practising in this country.

Charles Willson Peale

A prolific portrait-painter of Colonial and Revolutionary days, Charles Willson Peale was commissioned as early as 1772 by George Washington to paint the latter's likeness in miniature for Mrs. Washington. Two replicas of the ivory were made for the Custis children. One of these miniatures is now owned by Mr. William B. Osgood Field.

Small in size and generally showing the sitter almost full-face, Willson Peale's miniatures, though virtually never signed, are easy to identify. The heads are always well set off by the backgrounds, and the features are accurately drawn and in strong relief, the coloring being confined to a neutral key unrelieved by high or low notes. One feels that as likenesses they are often accurate enough, though uninspired. In his several miniatures of Washington, however, there is little or no resemblance to other portraits by better artists; and, as stated elsewhere, this is true of his Washington portraits in oil as well.

Peale's technic is admirably adapted to the diminutive size in which he customarily worked, and his ivories achieve in consequence a certain perfection artistically that contributes materially to their interest and value. The division of space ordinarily gives from a third to a half for the head; and the lips are usually on a line that would divide the oval almost exactly in half.

About 1790, Willson Peale discontinued painting in miniature professionally, and referred his customers to his younger brother, James. However, he still painted an occasional ivory, and continued to do so until as late as 1795.

Henry Pelham

Son of one of our earliest portrait-painters in oil, and stepbrother of John Singleton Copley, Henry Pelham received instruction in painting from both his father and his stepbrother. It was from the latter, unquestionably, that he learned the intricacies of painting in miniature, and the finish of his rare works in that branch of portraiture attests to the effectiveness of Copley's instruction. The few ivories which have so far been identified as from his hand are painted with a skill equal to the necessities of realizing with impeccable precision the likeness and character of the sitter, and of handling the light and shadow and the color in the face with sufficient sensitiveness and delicacy to give the likeness something of the luminosity of a living personality.

Pelham ranks with the best of our miniaturists, so far as we can determine from his known works; but these are so few in number that there is a natural hesitation about bracketing him with such masters as Copley, E. G. Malbone, Charles Fraser, and James Peale, lest later discoveries reveal less finished examples of his art to challenge our evaluation of his merit as a miniaturist. On the evidence of the three specimens which are all that are now known, he certainly reached a mastery of the art surpassed by but few of his contemporaries. The "Stephen Hooper" at the Metropolitan Museum of Art in New York, and the "William Wignall Stevens" and "Jonathan Clark" at the Museum of Fine Arts in Boston, are all ivories of conspicuous quality, and prove that at his best Pelham could paint a miniature as fine in its way as those of the better-known and more prolific artists above mentioned.

James Peale

James Peale was one of the best of our miniaturists, second only to Edward Greene Malbone at the end of the eighteenth century, and his considerable contribution to our native product of portraiture in little is among the chief glories of our artistic past. His ivories have an exuberance of coloring, and the faces a liveliness of expression, that particularly recommend them to the spectator. The coloring, covering a range unequaled by that of any other American miniaturist, is definitely an attraction of indubitable force; and the feeling realized in the faces—such as the disdain in the "Mrs. Hulings," the youthful happiness in the "Jacob Hull" with the dimple showing in his cheek, and the effectual feminine charm of the "Mrs. McCluney," the "Elizabeth Snyder," and the "Mrs. Van Ness"—help to make his product almost unique in a sense as obvious to the layman as to either artist or critic.

Peale's ivories are invariably oval. The smaller one measure one and three quarters by one and three eighths inches, while the larger run to three by two and a half inches or a trifle more. A great many are dated and signed "J P." In Peale's time the length of the vertial stroke of the "P" must have been intended to indicate that the single stroke of the first letter stood for "J" rather than for "I." If it were an "I" both it and the vertical line of the second initial would have been much shorter.

As noted earlier in this volume, one finds in James Peale's portraits of women a curious tendency to narrow the shoulders, which sometimes, as in the "Mrs. Copper," quite effectually defeats the truth of nature, and results in an inartistic picture unworthy of the painter. It was a definite failing, and in a less exaggerated degree it is noticeable in virtually all of his likenesses of women, and in some of the portraits of men as well. His miniatures are perhaps not so exquisite in technic as either Edward Greene Malbone's or Charles Fraser's, but they are painted with a verve and freedom foreign to the precision that characterizes the style of those masters. What Peale's miniatures lack in the delicacy of modeling and the sensitiveness and fineness of drawing which we see in the works of Malbone and

Fraser is offset to an appreciable degree by a heightened sense of living reality in more forcible rendering of feeling in his faces, and a superior range and brilliance of color.

Peale tried many forms of graphic art—landscape and historical composition as well as portraiture in oil—but eventually he devoted himself almost exclusively to miniature-painting. Ivories from his hand may be seen at the Metropolitan Museum of Art in New York and the Carnegie Museum in Pittsburgh.

William Verstille

One of the eighteenth-century miniaturists, William Verstille, whose works are very rare, worked in Boston and Salem, Massachusetts, and, later, in Philadelphia in 1782, and in New York in 1790. In the latter cities it is probable that he painted a number of officers of the Continental forces, as well as some prominent civilians.

The unique signed and dated "Edward Shaw," an oval ivory one and a half by one and three quarter inches in size, is set in a gold locket made by the miniaturist and goldsmith John Ramage. It has every appearance of being an accurate likeness, with the long nose unmodified by any attempt to subtract in the least from its dominance as an inartistic note. In more ways than one, it suggests Ramage's characteristic style; but the ivory is plainly signed above the sitter's left shoulder "W V pinx," and inscribed on the back "Painted by Wm. Verstille, New York, 15th May 1790." The technic is almost identical with that of Ramage, as well as the placing of the figure in the oval, and the pose—with the body and head turned slightly and the eyes fully open, looking to the spectator. However, the coloring of the background, a delicate reddish brown, is entirely different from Ramage's customary cool greens, grays, and blues.

Specimens of Verstille's work may be seen at the Essex Institute in Salem, Massachusetts.

John Trumbull

The miniatures in oil on wooden panels, about four inches high by three and a half inches wide, which John Trumbull painted, most of them as portrait studies for use in his larger historical composi-

Metropolitan Museum of Art, New York City

PLATE XLIV A

MARTIN VAN BUREN

By Henry Inman

Corcoran Art Gallery, Washington, D. C.

PLATE XLIV B

ASHER B. DURAND

By Charles Loring Elliott

tions, have the immediacy of appeal of intimate likenesses somewhat summarily executed. Most of those which he did in the early seventeen-nineties have light backgrounds; in the later ones, done after 1800, the backgrounds are dark. The miniatures of women are particularly lovely; and some of the military figures, such as the "Captain Seymour" and the "William Stevens," are exceedingly spirited in drawing.

Very wisely, Trumbull did not attempt to simulate the water-color effect of the true miniature on ivory, or to finish his little oils with anything approaching the elaboration of his larger canvases. It is precisely the offhand, sketchy quality of these small likenesses that constitutes their persuasive appeal. Gilbert Stuart's unfinished miniature of General Knox has much the same charm as Trumbull's "General Morgan," while for anything to compare with Trumbull's "Harriet and Sophia Chew," his "Julia Seymour," and his "Catherine Wadsworth" one must look to Edward Greene Malbone. On the other hand, the "John C. Calhoun," painted in 1827, is a more finished and less intriguing portrait in little. Nor are the likenesses of George and Martha Washington of more than secondary interest.

Trumbull's contribution to American miniature art is conspicuous by reason of being unique in material and method. He manages by suggestion to approach in effect the intricate elaboration of detail exhibited in the true miniature; whereas Albert Gallatin Hoit, a native artist of a later day, painted likenesses in oil on ivory quite in the manner of true miniatures, and with considerable success. Of course the smooth ivory surface helped Hoit to counterfeit the effect. Trumbull's wooden panels were less well adapted for this treatment, and he made no impossible demands upon his material.

These small oils of Trumbull's were made for a particular purpose in almost every instance, and not painted as commissions; thus he was fortunately able to do them to suit his own taste, and just how good a judge of art he was may be estimated by any one who examines them with the attention they deserve. Many will bracket them with the works of the best of our miniaturists, such as Malbone and Charles Fraser; and, making due allowance for the different

Yale Art Gallery, New Haven, Connecticut

PLATE XLV A

JOHN TRUMBULL

By Samuel L. Waldo

Detroit Institute of Arts, Detroit, Michigan

PLATE XLV B

MRS. EDWARD HUDSON

By Thomas Sully

medium, material, and manner, they undeniably belong in that company.

Joseph Dunkerley

Made at his home in North Square, Boston, in the seventeen-eighties, Joseph Dunkerley's miniatures are of sufficient merit to permit of their being mistaken for the work of John Singleton Copley. The single authenticated specimen of his product so far recorded, a likeness of Mary Burroughs, painted in 1787, which was shown at the Metropolitan Museum Exhibition of American Miniatures, in New York in 1927, conforms more to the style of John Ramage than to that of Copley.

The miniatures of Mr. and Mrs. Charles Bullfinch, attributed to Dunkerley by Mr. Wehle, are also more in the manner of Ramage than of Copley, but were probably by Dunkerley. The sitters were residents of Boston, and the ivories were painted in 1788, long after Copley and Ramage had left that city and just a year later than the Burroughs miniature.

Edward Savage

Better known for his large oil painting of the Washington family and his very unsuccessful portrait of George Washington painted for Harvard University, Edward Savage executed several quite competent miniatures, a self-portrait, a likeness of his wife Sarah, and one of his brother-in-law Eben Seaver. These miniatures are all in the permanent collection of the Art Museum in Worcester, Massachusetts, in the immediate vicinity of his birthplace, Princeton, Worcester County. They date from about 1794, when, returning from London, where he had studied with Benjamin West, Savage married in Boston, at the age of thirty-three, Sarah Seaver. The miniature he painted of the latter is a curiosity of composition, badly drawn, but with a remarkable fidelity in the delineation of costume and coiffure. His self-portrait, on the other hand, is probably the best of all his paintings, in either water-color or oil.

Robert Fulton

Specimens of the work in miniature of Robert Fulton, the inventor of the submarine, are to be seen at the Historical Society of Pennsylvania in Philadelphia, the Art Museum of Worcester, Massachusetts, and the New York Historical Society. Generally painted on rather large upright rectangular ivories, the later examples, such as that of his wife and the "Mrs. Van Rensselaer," are highly finished and attractive pictures, though hardly of a type to impress one very much as works of art, however beautiful. They have the appearance of "pretty girl" pictures.

Fulton had nothing like Edward Greene Malbone's or Charles Fraser's ability of infusing a face with the individual characteristics of the sitter. In consequence, he attains nothing but a more or less accurate rendering of features, very satisfactory in itself but devoid of any definite indication of character. It is a style of portraiture in little which George L. Saunders, who worked in Philadelphia and Baltimore in the eighteen-forties, carried to the limits of credulity. The portraits of the latter are about as nearly related to art as are the colored chromos of the present-day illustrator.

Archibald Robertson

Archibald Robertson, a Scotch miniaturist who settled in New York in 1791, painted a portrait of President Washington upon a small square of marble, and a number of ivories, including two self-portraits. His technic is admirable, and his portraits have a certain unconstrained air of simplicity that recommends them in any company. Three of his ivories, as well as the water-color of Washington on marble, may be seen at the New York Historical Society.

Benjamin Trott

A native miniaturist who failed by a very narrow margin to reach the distinction of ranking with the best of his contemporaries was Benjamin Trott. His portraits are forthright representations of his sitters, and have every appearance of being excellent likenesses. He copied on ivory a number of Gilbert Stuart's oils, in Philadelphia, where he worked for a time in the studio of Thomas Sully. In 1796 he was working with Elkanah Tisdale in Albany, New York, to which city he returned in 1826. He prac-

Museum of Fine Arts, Boston, Massachusetts

PLATE XLVI

GILBERT STUART

By John Neagle

tised in New York City in 1793, 1829–30, and 1832–33; in Charleston, South Carolina, in 1819; in Boston in 1833; and in Baltimore in 1839–41.

Trott used various technics—wash, line, hatching, and stippling; but certain characteristics of his faces (for instance, the rather high brow), of background (which is almost invariably light), and of color (in which he was notably deficient), help one to identify his work. His heads are well drawn, but the faces are not very successfully modeled, having an effect of flatness, save in a few exceptional cases such as the "Nicholas Biddle," probably his finest work, and the "Abner LeGrand."

Although Gilbert Stuart is reported to have preferred Trott's copies of his oils to those made by Walter Robertson, William Dunlap says that Trott was enamored of Robertson's coloring and that he (Dunlap) had seen in Trott's possession one of Robertson's miniatures half obliterated by experiments undertaken in an effort to discover the secret of Robertson's effects. Trott never succeeded in the effort, nor had he sufficient confidence to determine upon a technic adapted to his individual abilities and to develop a distinct type of portraiture in little.

But ability he certainly had, as his finer ivories amply prove. An example of his work may be seen at the Metropolitan Museum of Art in New York City.

William Dunlap

The best of William Dunlap's portraiture is in miniature, where in several instances (for example, the "John Park" at the New York Historical Society) he managed to create little masterpieces. His more ambitious ivories, however, are generally failures artistically, for the simple reason that he struggled with them too much in an effort to approximate a degree of excellence utterly beyond his abilities. When he confines himself to the simple task of painting directly an accurate likeness, without any attempt to imitate the perfection of technic which one associates particularly with miniature art, he is measurably successful within the limitations of an uninvolved style. But to delicate gradations of hue, as well as the finer shades of modeling in faces, he was entirely unequal, either in the small compass of a miniature or in the ample area of a canvas.

Worcester Art Museum, Worcester, Massachusetts

PLATE XLVII

JONATHAN BROOKS

By James Frothingham

Edward Greene Malbone

An illegitimate son of John Malbone of Newport, Rhode Island, carefully brought up in the privacy of his home, Edward Greene Malbone lived long enough to persuade the legislature of his State, by the brilliancy of his artistic success as a portrait miniaturist, to legitimatize him and his four brothers and sisters.

As a child Malbone colored engravings; in his boyhood he painted scenery for the local theater; and in 1794, when but seventeen, he left home and established himself professionally in the neighboring city of Providence, where he practised successfully. Thereafter he worked in Boston, New York, Philadelphia, and Charleston, South Carolina, and in the course of less than fifteen years became the American master of miniature-painting and one of the greatest of all miniaturists. His ivories are so meticulously painted as in many instances to conceal absolutely from the naked eye virtually all evidence of the minute hatching which he used. His color has a purity and clarity unmodified by either shading or effusion of light. The precision of his drawing and the accuracy of his modeling approach an almost photographic certitude.

With his friend Washington Allston he went in 1800 to Charleston, where he met and became the friend of Charles Fraser, with whom he corresponded thereafter. In May, 1801, he sailed with Allston for England, where he met Benjamin West and studied for a time at the Royal Academy schools. Unusually handsome, with charming manners and an equable temperament, he was much sought after socially. His engagements, however, were never allowed to interfere with his work, and he habitually spent eight hours a day at his easel or drawing-board. Eventually, this devotion to his art and the confinement and intense application it entailed broke his strength, and his naturally frail constitution was not equal to recuperating from that setback. He went to Jamaica in 1806 in a vain search for health; returning the next year, he landed at Savannah, Georgia, where he died at the home of his cousin, Robert Mackay, on May 7.

The finest of Malbone's ivories, such as the "Rebecca Gratz," the "Ralph Stead Izard," the

"Mrs. Gulian Verplanck," the "David Moses," the "Mrs. Alexander Bleecker," the "Mrs. James Lowndes," and the "Joseph Kirk Milnor," are privately owned, but good examples of his work may be seen at the Art Museum in Worcester, Massachusetts, the Metropolitan Museum of Art in New York, the Pennsylvania Museum in Philadelphia, and the Rhode Island School of Design in Providence.

Benjamin West in 1801 encouraged Malbone to remain in London, assuring him of success, and told James Monroe, then on his way to France, "I have seen a picture by a young man of the name of Malbone, which no man in England could excel." The daughters of Colonel Scolbay of Boston, a miniature of whom Malbone painted, told the artist's sister, Mrs. Whitehorne, that Gilbert Stuart visited them at least once a year to see the ivory, begging them to take great care of it, as it was decidedly the finest miniature in the world. Henry T. Tuckerman, in his "American Artist Life," tells of a foreign artist who recognized, in one of Malbone's miniatures of a girl of seventeen, the features of an old lady to whom he had been introduced a few days before.

Malbone's ivories are generally of medium size, from two and a half by two to three and a half by two and a half inches, with dark or light backgrounds of neutral coloring. Many of them he signed either in script or in small block letters, in various ways, as follows:

(1) E. G. M.
(2) MALBONE
(3) E. G. MALBONE
(4) EDW. G. MALBONE
(5) EDWARD G. MALBONE

Rembrandt Peale

One of the several sons of Charles Willson Peale, Rembrandt Peale, though primarily a portrait-painter in oil, at the beginning of his professional career, in the seventeen-nineties, made a number of miniatures on ivory of rather generous proportions. These works, often signed with his initials "R.P.," and dated, are for the most part rather florid in color, and too prosaically realistic ever to achieve artistic success, whatever their merit as likenesses.

John Wesley Jarvis

Early in the nineteenth century—in 1804, to be exact—John Wesley Jarvis began to paint miniatures in partnership with Joseph Wood in New York City, sharing a studio with that artist, where both received some assistance from Edward Greene Malbone in the course of a visit the latter paid them in company with William Dunlap. In 1809 the partnership of Jarvis and Wood was dissolved, and the following year Jarvis visited Charleston, South Carolina; in 1811 he was in Baltimore, and in 1813 and 1814 he exhibited in Philadelphia, though there is no certainty of his having painted miniatures in those cities.

The scarcity of Jarvis's ivories makes it seem more than likely that he practised portrait-painting in oil rather than in miniature after about 1810. His miniature of his sister may be seen at the Rhode Island School of Design in Providence, and a signed miniature of an unidentified man, dated 1809, at the Metropolitan Museum of Art in New York City.

Elkanah Tisdale

Elkanah Tisdale, one of the considerable school of Connecticut copper-plate engravers, drew admirable small portraits in pencil and painted a number of very creditable miniatures, working in New York City in 1805 and visiting Albany, New York, with Benjamin Trott in 1826 and 1827. His ivories are not so free in treatment as Trott's, and in coloring and style resemble more closely the work of Anson Dickinson. They are generally unsigned, but are sometimes mounted with Tisdale's business card in the back. Examples may be seen at the New Haven Colony Historical Society, and the Connecticut Historical Society at Hartford.

Anson Dickinson

Working first as a silversmith in Litchfield, Connecticut, Anson Dickinson began to paint miniatures professionally about 1804, and was practising in Albany, New York, as early as 1805. In 1811, according to William Dunlap, he was the foremost miniaturist in New York City. In 1818 he went to Canada; he settled in New Haven, Connecticut, in

1840, but in 1847 removed to Hartford, where he died.

Most of Dickinson's ivories are of medium size, about three by two and a half inches, and generally unsigned, though some have his business card framed in the back. The best of them are exquisite in color and finished with superior technical skill. He was, however, uneven in his work, and many of his miniatures are so utterly lacking in the qualities that distinguish his finer ones as to be hardly recognizable. His "Gilbert Stuart" is at the New York Historical Society, his "Mrs. Robert Watts" at the Metropolitan Museum of Art in New York; but in order to see him at his best, one should visit the Historical Society at Litchfield, Connecticut, where several of his finest works are preserved.

Charles Fraser

Though his "Jane Winthrop" dates from 1802, when he was but twenty, before Charles Fraser made painting his profession he studied for the law. He was admitted to the bar in 1807, and practised successfully in Charleston, South Carolina, his native city, until 1818. By that time he had accumulated a competency, and the remainder of his life he devoted to art, painting miniatures professionally until as late as 1852. He was the first to instruct Thomas Sully in the rudiments of art, though himself a mere boy at the time. Later, through Washington Allston, a South Carolinian also, he became acquainted with Edward Greene Malbone, whose friendship and devotion to miniature art must have been a very strong influence in the development of Fraser's taste.

Beginning to work in miniature when thirty-six years of age, Fraser ranks second among native miniaturists. The rather coarse hatching and stippling in his ivories is characteristic of his style. It was, we must believe, deliberately adopted to meet a slight weakening of sight as he aged, and was developed to a point where it enabled him to realize a degree of excellence in his little portraits that accords them a place among the masterpieces of the greatest miniaturists. His self-portrait of 1823, the "Elizabeth Sarah Faber" of 1846, the "Charles Winthrop" of 1827, and the "Francis Kinloch Huger" of 1825 are well-nigh perfect examples of portraiture in little. The "Elizabeth Sarah Faber" is especially charm-

Metropolitan Museum of Art, New York City

PLATE XLVIII

SELF-PORTRAIT

By John Vanderlyn

ing, with its delicate color scheme of soft grays and blues, fine flesh tones, utter simplicity of design, sensitively modeled features, and beautifully drawn figure.

Fraser was, if anything, more successful even than Malbone in incorporating in a face the evidence of a sitter's character. In every ivory from his hand one recognizes a distinct personality whose traits are clearly indicated, the features and expression conspiring to produce a speaking likeness. Malbone was generally content with suggesting the character of a sitter, and then embroidering thereon in exquisite touches until the portrait realized an artistic ideal rather than an exact likeness.

Though Fraser continued to work in miniature long after the introduction of photography, the productions of the camera seem never to have affected his manner of painting, and his later ivories have the same characteristics that are found in the early examples, the only noticeable change in method being the above-mentioned enlargement of the hatching and stippling. More than three hundred of his miniatures were shown in the Fraser Gallery exhibition of 1857, which he assembled in Charleston, and virtually twice as many of his ivories are known to-day as of any other American artist. Miniatures by Fraser may be seen at the Boston Museum of Fine Arts, the Worcester Art Museum, and the Metropolitan Museum in New York City.

Thomas Sully

Virtually all of the miniatures of Thomas Sully were painted in the first years of the last century. The artist studied with a French miniaturist in the South before 1800, and his work in the field of miniature-painting shows the influence of the Frenchman's instruction. He never succeeded in making more than a minor impression with his work, though he painted many ivories before 1810, and eventually he gave up painting on ivory altogether and devoted himself to portraiture in oil, in which he achieved a great popular success before 1850.

Matthew Harris Jouett

In the first years of his professional life as a lawyer in Lexington, Kentucky, Matthew Harris Jouett devoted his leisure to the painting of miniatures on ivory, especially delighting in female portraiture, of

Cleveland Museum of Art, Cleveland, Ohio

PLATE XLIX

JAMES G. MC KINNEY

By Matthew Harris Jouett

which he was so enamored that frequent and protracted sittings were the only compensation he asked for his early ivories. Some of these works are surprisingly beautiful; indeed, they are so fine that a contemporary miniaturist of repute in Philadelphia could hardly believe that they were the work of a self-taught backwoodsman.

General Samuel W. Price, in his "Old Masters of the Bluegrass," lists eighteen ivories by Jouett, but there are probably at least four or five times that number. He had an individual and characteristic technic, especially noticeable in his miniatures, which, instead of being in the conventional manner, stippled and hatched, were executed more in the broad style of oil portraiture, with frequent washes. His backgrounds are very simply treated, all accessories are subordinated, and little attention is given to dress even in his portraits of women. Virtually all of his miniatures are privately owned in Kentucky.

Nathaniel Rogers

A student of Joseph Wood (who was for some time the partner of John Wesley Jarvis), Nathaniel Rogers was one of the few artists whose miniatures continued to be worthy of attention as works of art after the introduction of the daguerreotype. Beginning to practise about 1810 in New York City, he became a member of the National Academy, where he exhibited a frame of four ivories as late as 1827, and continued to paint in miniature until the early eighteen-thirties.

Rogers's miniatures lack the essential elegance of technic and the intriguing color which are almost a necessity of portraiture in little; the faces are more or less expressionless, but they still present interesting and attractive features sufficient to merit some praise. A good pair, the likenesses of Mr. and Mrs. Charles T. Savage, may be seen at the Art Museum in Worcester, Massachusetts.

Samuel F. B. Morse

As a student at Yale College, Samuel F. B. Morse painted miniatures on ivory (the sitter furnishing the ivory) for five dollars each, helping in that way to meet his expenses. No examples of his work at this period have been identified so far. Sometime about 1815, however, he painted in Concord, New Hampshire, a rather large upright rectangular ivory of

Miss Lucretia Pickering Walker, whom he met there and later married. It is a fine work in the rather "beautified" style of his later portraiture in oil, though looser and more freely brushed. Its likeness to his oils consists mainly in the elaborate costume, and the extreme care with which it is rendered. The pose is somewhat more artificial, though happily the composition is simpler, resulting in a more artistic effect. The face is altogether lovely, expressive and alight with feeling.

As Morse's ivories are unsigned, one is forced in attributing ivories to him to substantiate conclusions by a painstaking study of the few identified miniatures and an inferential theory of the probable development of his technic in his later works.

Anna Claypoole Peale

Anna Claypoole Peale was the daughter of James Peale, one of the best of our early miniaturists, and the granddaughter of James Claypoole, a Colonial portrait-painter in oil, so she had a double inheritance of artistic talent. She studied with her father, and in her early twenties began painting in miniature professionally. Her ivories in which the backgrounds are lighter in tone, frequently of blue cloud-flecked sky, the style unstudied and the brushing free, have a definite charm, though they rarely reach a degree of finish that would justify unqualified approval. In technic she resorted to wash rather than to stippling or hatching, and her coloring covers a considerable range, which gives her works a variety of interest. Her ivories are ovals of about the customary size, three by two and a half inches or two and a half by two and a quarter inches, and are generally signed and dated, the signature usually reading "Anna C. Peale."

This artist did almost all of her work in Philadelphia and Baltimore and the near-by country, during the first half of the nineteenth century. Her portraiture seems not to have been affected in any way by the advent of photography, and maintained its original characteristics to the end of her career.

Robert Field

All of the known works produced in this country by Robert Field, an English artist, save a few watercolor likenesses, were ivories painted in and near Washington, D. C., and the neighboring State of

Museum of Fine Arts, Boston, Massachusetts

PLATE L

SELF-PORTRAIT

By Washington Allston

Maryland. Field must be ranked with the best of our native miniaturists. His portraits are executed with remarkable precision and exquisite realization of insubstantial subtleties of color and values. His faces have an air of living reality, so alight are they with human feeling. His technic approaches the perfection of Edward Greene Malbone's in its refinement, his stippling and hatching being inconspicuous in the sense that they must always be in a finished work of art.

He painted a number of miniatures of George Washington for Mrs. Washington in 1800 and 1801, after Washington's death, basing them upon one of Gilbert Stuart's portraits of the Vaughn type, with variations suggested by Mrs. Washington. The few of these that have not lost a great measure of their original fine color suggest that his own portraiture, at least in miniature, is preferable. None of these ivories reach the distinction of his representations of Miss Henrietta Sprigg, Mrs. Mary Tayloe Lloyd Key, and the youthful Charles Ridgely.

Field worked in the United States for but a few years, approximately from 1794 to 1806, and painted in miniature and water-color exclusively so far as is known, finishing more than seventy ivories, sixty-four of which are listed in Mr. Harry Piers's exhaustive biographical and critical monograph on the artist, published several years ago. Field later worked for a number of years in Canada, where he painted both miniatures and oil portraits.

George Catlin

Better known as the author and illustrator of an important book on the North American Indian, George Catlin painted miniatures as well as portraits in oil. He worked in Philadelphia, New York City, Hartford, Connecticut, and Albany, New York, in the first third of the nineteenth century. His miniatures are conspicuous for the fact that the size of the head, in proportion to the surface of the ivory, is generally much exaggerated. Nor are his portraits either good enough in color or fine enough in technic to achieve more than ordinary success; their chief interest centers about the personalities of his sitters; among whom were Governor DeWitt Clinton, Dolly Madison, and other important figures of Catlin's time.

Thomas B. Clarke Collection

PLATE LI A

WILLIAM WIRT

By Chester Harding

Property of Frederic Fairchild Sherman, Westport, Connecticut

PLATE LI B

JONATHAN JEUE

By John Paradise

Thomas Sier Cummings

A student of Henry Inman, the portrait-painter in oil, Thomas Sier Cummings devoted himself from about 1826 exclusively to the painting of miniatures, practising mainly in New York City, where he was very active in the affairs of the National Academy. His ivories range from one and a half by one inch to very generous proportions, and are both oval and rectangular in form. Technically, they are satisfactory though uninteresting. Cummings seldom succeeded in producing anything better than an acceptable likeness or achieving other than a commonplace effect. A good draftsman and a competent painter, he was not really an artist in the higher sense, at all.

Henry Colton Shumway

In the South, Charles Fraser, and in the North, Henry Colton Shumway, were the last of the early school of native miniaturists. The citizens of Charleston, South Carolina, where Fraser lived and worked, and of the adjacent territory, with commendable pride in his talent supplied him with commissions sufficient to keep him busy until his death in 1860. Shumway, who in the eighteen-thirties was probably the most popular and successful miniaturist in the great city of New York, was not so fortunate. After the Civil War, when the daguerreotype had reduced the demand for miniatures, he was forced to resort to tinting photographs in order to make a living.

Shumway was born in Middletown, Connecticut, but went to New York in 1827. He studied at the National Academy, and in 1829 began to paint professionally. He was made a member of the Academy in 1832, at the height of his career. Most of his ivories are of generous proportions, rectangular in form, with modulated backgrounds of neutral hues in a rather large stipple. Their coloring is rich though reserved in effect. Most of his works are signed on the face or inscribed in ink on the back, his signature on the painted side being scratched in script and reading simply "Shumway." His faces are brushed in with something of the freedom of oil painting, the method being wash rather than stipple. Hatching is entirely foreign to his practice, so far as may be ascertained from examination of known examples of his work.

As likenesses Shumway's portraits have an air of faithfully reproducing the most minute characteristics of a sitter, and their accuracy of representation constitutes their chief title to distinction. One recognizes in the best of his miniatures personalities as varied and as interesting as those one meets in everyday life. His "Cyrus W. Field" may be seen at the United States National Museum in Washington, D. C., but the majority of his ivories are still privately owned, presumably treasured by the descendants of the sitters.

PART V

LANDSCAPE-PAINTERS

LIST OF PAINTERS

John Trumbull	American	1756–1843
Washington Allston	American	1779–1843
Thomas Birch	English	1779–1851
Samuel L. Waldo	American	1783–1861
Thomas Doughty	American	1793–1856
William Jewett	American	1795–1874
Asher B. Durand	American	1796–1886
Thomas Cole	English	1801–1848
John F. Kensett	American	1818–1872
Frederick E. Church	American	1826–1900

New Milford Historical Society, New Milford, Connecticut

PLATE LII

JUDGE DAVID SHERMAN BOARDMAN

Painted in 1853 by Samuel L. Waldo and William Jewett

PART V

LANDSCAPE-PAINTERS

About 1760, Thomas Pownal, Colonial Governor of Massachusetts, made topographical drawings which were afterward reproduced in oils by Paul Sandby, an English artist. In 1768, Christian Remick, who came from Spain but certainly was not Spanish, painted water-color views of Boston Harbor. An artist named Albert C. Pleasants, of whom no biographical data are obtainable, painted in 1795 a "View of Richmond, Virginia," as seen from the falls in the James River.

Aside from the work of these three men, there was no landscape-painting in America until the end of the eighteenth century, when Ralph Earl, a native artist, painted the large canvas "Looking East from Leicester Hills," a view over what is now the city of Worcester, Massachusetts. Indeed, Thomas Cole, Thomas Doughty, and Frederick E. Church, all of the early nineteenth century, are in reality the first of our landscape school proper. Beginning with the grandiose conceptions of Cole and Church, with their vast distances and their emphasis upon the sublimity of nature, the early development of landscape-painting was toward a more accurate and painstaking rendering of detail, as seen in the canvases of the Hudson River School.

At first, when the classics were still common reading in our homes, scenes of heroic splendor and tragic significance, such as Cole's "Course of Empire" and "Voyage of Life," Washington Allston's "Deluge," and Church's "Ægean Sea," were of the type in vogue. Later, while the view remained extensive, interest was centered in nature itself, and the canvases became more truly representative of the American scene—though painters of the early school, such as John Trumbull, still preferred the magnificence of Niagara Falls to the more characteristic views of valley, hill, and farm land. As a consequence, nearly all of the early native landscapes are quite large; and, owing to the lack of space in most public galleries, but few of them are exhibited to-day.

The historical importance of these works is not adequately estimated. It is actually impossible to

Property of Miss Jeanette L. Gaylord, Kent, Connecticut

PLATE LIII

REBECCA JEWETT

Painted in 1842 by William S. Jewett

form any correct idea of the development of landscape-painting in this country without familiarity with its beginnings. Nor are the canvases without real merit within the limitations of their obvious intention, which was to impress one with the magnitude of the human struggle and the grandeur of the scene in which it was set. Whatever they lacked in intriguing color and inviting aspect, they were definitely moving in their effect upon the emotions. One is still conscious to-day of a direct reaction to the dramatic significance and tragic possibilities of nature and of life—the basic idea upon which they were built. In place of this, we are now seemingly satisfied with the subtleties of a persuasive but much less vigorous and vital portrayal of nature.

It is easy to dismiss with faint praise the patent and inescapable inferences of such a composition as Allston's "Deluge," but it is not so easy to reconstruct from our imagination a scene of similar graphic lucidity; and this is quite as true of the works of Cole and Church. Whether one does or does not care for them in no wise affects their artistic merit as examples of a mode of graphic expression which has its own importance; and they are too important in the history of American painting to be slighted or overlooked in the study of native art.

John Trumbull

It is not very generally realized that John Trumbull, who was preëminently a portraitist and historical painter, found time to paint several large pictures of Niagara Falls. His success in their composition, however, was not sufficient to encourage him to further efforts in that direction, and only a few canvases remain to remind us of his excursion into the field of landscape. Several of these paintings are to be seen at the New York Historical Society.

Washington Allston

A few landscapes from the hand of Washington Allston remain as impressive mementoes of his travels abroad. The "Swiss Scenery," simple in design and dignified in color, achieves something of the impressiveness of the mountain landscape. His "Alpine Scenery," a composition of similar character, was eventually ruined, in the opinion of the artist, by a professional restorer in Boston. Besides these two canvases he painted a picture of Mount Vesuvius.

Thomas Birch

Though more often thought of as a historical painter, Thomas Birch painted many Hudson River landscapes and views along the Schuykill. He was a competent draftsman, and these canvases are satisfactory representations of actual scenes, though entirely lacking any touch of inspiration in either design or coloring. Naturally, even in the artist's own time they failed more or less to make any sort of impression beside the finer work of Thomas Doughty and Thomas Cole.

Samuel L. Waldo

Probably it is not generally known to-day that Samuel L. Waldo painted both still life and landscape. As a matter of fact, as late as 1820, long after he was a well-established and successful portrait-painter in New York, he exhibited a landscape at the American Academy of Art. No example of his landscape-painting seems to be preserved in any of our museums or galleries to-day, and it is therefore impossible to describe their characteristics, but it is quite safe to take for granted that they exhibited definite merits.

Thomas Doughty

We may say that Thomas Doughty, born in Philadelphia in 1793, was the father of American landscape, though it was not until about 1823 that he gave up his business as a manufacturer of leather goods to devote his attention to art, and he always spoke scornfully of his first attempts as a painter. His only preparation seems to have been a single quarter's instruction in drawing, and probably his early pictures in oil were pretty bad. He later made something of a reputation by painting small, picturesque, and nicely colored native scenes.

Doughty's fame rests upon the series of landscapes of generous proportions which followed. In them we discover the models for Thomas Cole's and Frederick E. Church's compositions. Doughty had a natural aptitude for effective design, and his pictures, however extensive the view, are impressive because of the dignity that results therefrom, and which sufficiently substantiates their truth to nature.

His limitations have to do with personal, emo-

PLATE LIV

Top—SELF-PORTRAIT
By John Singleton Copley
Property of Mr. Henry Copley Greene, Boston, Massachusetts

Center—WILLIAM WIGNALL STEVENS
By Henry Pelham
Museum of Fine Arts, Boston

Bottom—MRS. MICHAEL TANEY
By Charles Willson Peale
Property of Mr. R. T. H. Halsey, Annapolis, Md.

Top—PENELOPE DWELLY
By John Singleton Copley
The Henry Walters Collection, New York City

Center—STEPHEN HOOPER
By Henry Pelham
Metropolitan Museum, New York City

Bottom—MAJOR WILLIAM JACKSON
By Charles Willson Peale
Collection of Independence Hall, Philadelphia

tional expression, in which his landscape is notably deficient. He was a master in recording the actual aspect of scenery, but lacked inspiration sufficient to imbue his landscape with human interest. He painted "The Hudson River," "The Delaware Water-Gap," and many similar canvases of large size. Examples of his work may be seen at the Metropolitan Museum of Art in New York City, the Pennsylvania Academy in Philadelphia, and the Boston Athenæum.

William Jewett

Though William Jewett spent the greater part of his active life as an artist painting portraits in partnership with his master, Samuel L. Waldo, while still a pupil in Waldo's studio he exhibited a landscape at the American Academy in 1820. He was originally a carriage-painter in New London, Connecticut, and landscapes and figure compositions were more within his grasp as a student; it was not until the influence of Waldo became effective that he devoted his attention exclusively to portraiture. His bust of Asher B. Durand as a young man, exhibited in 1819, was the first work of its kind from his hand.

Asher B. Durand

Having already made a considerable reputation both as an engraver and a portrait-painter, Asher B. Durand for over forty years, dating from 1839, painted landscape almost exclusively. His pictures, for the most part portraits of individual trees, have never been surpassed in their way. According to the artist's son, it was Durand's practice "while painting faithfully what he saw, not to paint all that he saw. From a group of trees he would select one that seemed, in age, color, or form, to be the most characteristic of its species, or, in other words, the most beautiful. In painting its surroundings, he eliminated all shrubs and other trees which interfered with the impression made by this one. Every outdoor study, as well as every pictorial composition, he treated as a sort of dramatic scene in which a particular tree or aspect of nature may be called the principal figure; other trees, as in the case of a study, being subordinate and of relative value in giving the most interesting object strong relief." These portraits of trees are Durand's finest works in oil and achieve an almost human significance.

PLATE LV

Top—MRS. JOHN PINTARD
By John Ramage
New York Historical Society

Center—JOHN MC CLUNEY
By James Peale
The Henry Walters Collection

Bottom—REBECCA GRATZ
By Edward Greene Malbone
Property of Miss Rachel Gratz Nathan

Top—JOHN PINTARD
By John Ramage
New York Historical Society

Center—MRS. JOHN MC CLUNEY
By James Peale
The Henry Walters Collection

Bottom—RALPH STEAD IZARD
By Edward Greene Malbone
The Henry Walters Collection

Thomas Cole

Born in England in 1801, Thomas Cole came to this country with his parents in 1819 and settled first in Ohio, where he studied the rudiments of art with some unrecorded painter. He later studied abroad, but the greater part of his life he spent in New York, where in the scenery of the Hudson River and the Catskill Mountains he found the subjects for many of his most successful pictures. His conception of nature was primarily as the background of the human drama, and his pictures have something of the character of scenes of grandeur in which the figures introduced enact definite rôles.

So far as it is unique in the field of painting, this type of landscape painted by Cole must be approached with an open mind and studied seriously before its merits or its defects can be accurately estimated. Our tendency in looking at a picture is to judge it entirely from a personal and perhaps opposite point of view from that which the artist chose in painting it. In the last analysis, it is only by discovering the artist's intention that we can understand a work of art and arrive at a competent judgment of its failure or success. It is a common characteristic of modern criticism to rely too much upon current standards of artistic creation and expression, and to substitute for actual knowledge of obsolete forms established opinions, whether right or wrong. It is possible that, in its way and of its kind, the landscape of Thomas Cole is quite as noteworthy as that of George Inness or of Dwight Tryon—to mention but two of our more recent landscape-painters.

John F. Kensett

John F. Kensett was born in Connecticut in 1818. He studied engraving with his uncle, Alfred Daggett, and while occupied with the laborious detail incident to that art turned his attention to painting in oils as a recreation. His progress, together with his ardent love of nature, led him eventually to abandon engraving entirely for landscape-painting. He said that his "real life commenced in England in the stately woods of Windsor, and the beeches of Burnham, and the lovely and fascinating landscape that surrounds them." His earliest canvases are devoted to these scenes. Later, upon his return from abroad, he explored and pictured the mountains of New

England and the Adirondacks, the seacoast at Newport, Lake George, and the Hudson and Genesee rivers.

Unlike Thomas Doughty and Thomas Cole, Kensett seldom resorted to an extensive view or a dramatic one as the basis for a picture, however large. He relied rather upon a sensitive realization of transitory atmospheric effects for that beauty which is so much a part of his artistic creation. In his work one observes the delicate transcription of themes of elusive color in subtle chromatic harmonies which furnishes the inspiration for our landscape-painters of a later generation. He links them to the first native practitioners in this field—men like Frederick E. Church, who frequently touched a chord of harmony, and Cole and Doughty, who infrequently touched a deeper note from the harp of the skies.

Kensett's finest canvases are those in which one finds the most subtle renderings of a chromatic theme, often in a single hue, like the gray of a sky, the gold of a sunset, the reds of autumn foliage, or the green of water. Sometimes in these pictures he almost reminds one of the monochrome ceramics of the ancient Chinese. Though a sort of early Flemish fidelity to the most infinitesimal detail marks certain passages in some of his canvases, in others everything else is entirely subordinated to a full realization of momentary effect of supreme atmospheric beauty.

Kensett was the greatest American landscape-painter of his time, and enjoyed a well-deserved success for many years preceding the rise in favor of the new type of landscape as painted by George Inness, Homer Martin, and Alexander Wyant.

Frederick E. Church

Frederick E. Church, born at Hartford, Connecticut, studied art in his own country and never went to Europe, though he traveled extensively in America. He was particularly successful in reproducing elusive atmospheric effects, as of snow, rain, clouds, mists, and rainbows. He chose as subjects for his canvases, volcanoes, icebergs, and waterfalls; and in his "Niagara" no less a critic of art than Ruskin remarked an effect of light upon water which he said he had frequently observed in nature.

Church's earlier pictures are faithful renderings of actual scenes, which he elaborated with an intention of illuminating them with the transcendent beauty of momentary and uncommon atmospheric conditions. Sky effects were his first triumphs in painting. His later works are more realistic in general effect, but are no less saturated with the prismatic glamour that pervades his early canvases. Whatever of inspiration he derived from his association with Thomas Cole, with whom he lived and studied for a time, his landscape is of an entirely different character than Cole's. It is uninvolved with sentiment. The human element, which Cole introduced in a leading rôle in many of his dramatic compositions, Church either left out of his pictures altogether or subordinated to a degree commensurate with its actual importance in relation to his subject.

PART VI

HISTORICAL PAINTERS

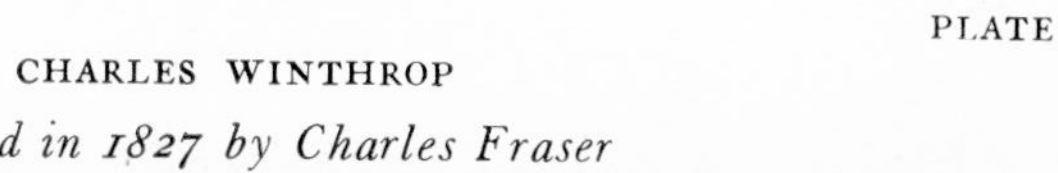

PLATE LVI A

CHARLES WINTHROP

Painted in 1827 by Charles Fraser

The Henry Walters Collection

PLATE LVI B

ELIZABETH SARAH FABER

Painted in 1846 by Charles Fraser

LIST OF PAINTERS

John Singleton Copley	American	1738–1815
Benjamin West	American	1738–1820
James Peale	American	1749–1831
Ralph Earl	American	1751–1801
John Trumbull	American	1756–1843
Elkanah Tisdale	American	1771 ——
John Vanderlyn	American	1775–1852
Rembrandt Peale	American	1778–1860
Thomas Birch	English	1779–1851
Samuel F. B. Morse	American	1791–1872
Asher B. Durand	American	1796–1886
Robert W. Weir	American	1803–1889
J. B. Stearnes	American	1810–1885
William Page	American	1811–1885
William Ranney	American	1813–1857
Tompkins H. Matteson	American	1813–1884
Edwin White	American	1817–1877
Charles Deas	American	1818–1867
Emanuel Leutze	German	1816–1869
George W. Flagg	American	1816–1897
Daniel Huntington	American	1816–1906

PLATE LVII

Top—HENRIETTA SPRIGG
By Robert Field
The Henry Walters Collection

Center—CORNELIA SCHUYLER, 1776–1808
Painted in 1792 by John Trumbull
The Yale Art Gallery

Bottom—EDWARD SHAW
By William Verstille
Ehrich Galleries, New York City

Top—DR. JAMES SERGEANT EWING
By Robert Field
Collection of Mr. Herbert L. Pratt, New York City

Center—THOMAS PINCKNEY 1750–1828
By John Trumbull

Bottom—SELF-PORTRAIT
By Edward Savage
Worcester Art Museum

PART VI

HISTORICAL PAINTERS

THE earliest historical pictures painted in America had to do entirely with the stirring events of the Revolution. In 1775, Ralph Earl painted views of the "Battle of Lexington," "Troops Destroying Stores in Concord," "The Battle at the North Bridge, Concord," and "The South Part of Lexington, where the First Detachment were joined by Lord Percy," all of which were engraved by Amos Doolittle. These compositions, though made on the sites of the various events, are commonplace representations, without any particular value in an artistic sense. Elkanah Tisdale painted, as a youth, a "Battle of Lexington," but the most pretentious and successful of these Revolutionary subjects was the series painted much later by John Trumbull. Thomas Birch, an Englishman, the son of a miniature-painter in enamel, is the only artist of an early date who celebrated the triumphs of the American Navy on the high seas.

John Singleton Copley

After he was settled in England, in the late seventeen-seventies, John Singleton Copley painted all of his historical canvases, which are concerned with English, not American, history. The first of these pictures was "The Death of Lord Chatham." Besides this work, Copley painted "The Defence of Gibraltar," "The Death of Major Pierson," "Charles the First in the House of Commons," and "The Surrender of Admiral De Winter." It was the first and second of these canvases that made Copley's reputation in London, where the remainder of his life was spent in the painting of portraits, which was his proper métier. He was not equal to creating a composition of impressive character involving the disposition of numerous figures, and his historical works are noteworthy only as collections of portraits of celebrated figures.

Benjamin West

The most prolific and one of the best of our native painters of historical scenes, classical, religious, and military, was Benjamin West, the American president of the Royal Academy in London at the end of the eighteenth century. One of his first works in this field—an American subject—was "Penn's Treaty with the Indians." Other canvases represented "The Death of Wolfe," "The Surrender of Calais," "The Death of Nelson," "The Battle of Cressy," "Installation of the Knights of the Garter," and "The Death of Chevalier Bayard." The classical subjects from his brush included "The Departure of Regulus from Rome," painted by royal command for the king.

All of these works were of heroic size, and their execution entailed effort commensurate with their proportions and comparable with the most ambitious performances of the Old Masters. That they are no longer esteemed in no wise proves that they are without human interest or artistic merit of a very high order. A number of West's important classical works are now owned in this country, including "The Death of Hyacinthus," "Venus Lamenting the Death of Adonis," and "Juno Presenting Arms to Venus."

James Peale

Although James Peale's reputation is exclusively that of a portrait-miniaturist, one of his earliest productions was a Revolutionary scene representing "The Death of General Mercer at Princeton."

Ralph Earl

In 1775, Ralph Earl was in active service in the Continental Army at Cambridge and Lexington, and soon thereafter he painted the several pictures of memorable events of the Revolution already referred to. These were probably the earliest historical compositions actually painted in America. They were engraved by Amos Doolittle of New Haven, Connecticut, who had served beside Earl in the Army and was the best of our early native engravers.

Though many of the Doolittle prints are extant, the present whereabouts of Earl's originals is unknown. The engravings, however, sufficiently indicate the character of the pictures, and we know that they were rather juvenile in effect—troops scattered

Worcester Art Museum, Worcester, Massachusetts

PLATE LVIII

LOOKING EAST FROM LEICESTER HILLS

By Ralph Earl

about and grouped like lead soldiers, and buildings which resemble houses built of blocks.

John Trumbull

In the effort to make his historical paintings accurate John Trumbull went to the infinite trouble of painting a long series of miniature portraits from life of officers of the enemy and Continental troops engaged, and civil authorities as well, so as to incorporate in his canvases faithful likenesses of all the important figures. The first of these compositions, the "Battle of Bunker Hill," was finished in Benjamin West's studio in London in 1786, where it was mistaken by Joshua Reynolds for West's work.

Trumbull was, of course, familiar with West's picture of "The Death of Wolfe" and with "The Death of Major Pierson," by John Singleton Copley, and he himself had already made a small sketch in ink of "The Death of General Frazer at Bemus's Heights." Perhaps unfortunately—at least for its popular success—Trumbull chose for his Bunker Hill picture the moment in which the enemy triumphed. Its accuracy has been questioned, and not without reason; but as a work of art it remains unquestionably the best of all the representations we have of that historic battle.

All of Trumbull's canvases were compositions on a miniature scale, intended for reproduction in engraving, and their size enhances rather than diminishes their effect as well as their charm. The larger replicas of some of them, eventually made for the Government and placed in the rotunda of the Capitol at Washington, are inferior in every respect to the originals now exhibited at the Yale Art Gallery, though they were shown with great success in various cities throughout the country soon after they were painted.

"The Death of Montgomery," the second of the series, also was painted in West's studio in London, in the three months following the completion of the first canvas. Thereafter Trumbull painted an English subject, the "Sortie of the Garrison of Gibraltar," which he gave to West, making a larger replica of it which he sold to Sir Francis Baring. The remaining pictures of the Revolutionary series, "The Declaration of Independence," "The Surrender of Burgoyne," "The Surrender of Cornwallis," and

Metropolitan Museum of Art, New York City

PLATE LIX

THE DELUGE

By Washington Allston

"The Resignation of Washington," selected by the American Congress, were painted in this country after 1816. All of these admirable compositions are more or less historically inaccurate in detail, according to their critics, but their merits so far overshadow whatever faults they may have that one is compelled to admit their obvious success in a difficult mode of artistic representation.

Of the portrait miniatures in oil upon little oval wooden panels, which Trumbull painted from life in order that the likenesses in his Revolutionary scenes might be accurate, it may safely be said that no finer miniatures of the kind have been painted since. If they had never found use in the larger groups on canvas, they would constitute in themselves a very precious contribution to American art. In construction, Trumbull managed in these scenes to place the emphasis always on the significant group about which the action of the moment is centered. In so doing, he translated the representation from the commonplace of a merely pictorial effect to the dignity of a truly artistic creation; and whatever their defects, nothing can defeat their success as really moving episodes.

Having served in the Continental Army, and being personally acquainted with many of the commanding officers and conversant with their descriptions of important engagements, Trumbull was better qualified than most of his critics to judge as to the propriety of his portrayals of these historic scenes. One cannot help admiring his disregard of public disapproval, and his insistence upon picturing each episode according to his own notion of its actual enactment. If in minor matters the paintings are inexact, in the larger and more important sense of truthfully picturing the events as a whole they are notably successful. Beside them, the engravings of Paul Revere appear grotesque, and those from the paintings of Ralph Earl and Elkanah Tisdale look like the productions of precocious children, picturing scenes beyond the limits of their immature understanding.

Elkanah Tisdale

Having served an apprenticeship as a painter in a carriage shop in Lebanon, Connecticut, where he was born, Elkanah Tisdale before receiving any real instruction in art appeared in Hartford in the early seventeen-nineties, with a large picture of the "Battle of Lexington." The painting, whatever its merits, enjoyed a popularity there at the time which led to its being almost immediately engraved. It seems to have been the artist's only historical picture. Unfortunately, its present location is not known.

John Vanderlyn

Though he is known to us to-day rather as a portrait-painter and for his famous study of the nude "Ariadne," John Vanderlyn as a young man painted several notable historical subjects such as "The Murder of Jane McCrea by the Indians," executed while the artist was abroad in 1803. In Paris he painted for one of the panels in the Capitol in Washington, D. C., "The Landing of Columbus," which Henry T. Tuckerman, an early art historian, dismisses as being "a respectable, rather than a great, picture," though he does say that it is "excellent in parts."

Rembrandt Peale

Among the almost unknown works of Rembrandt Peale is a painting of the American frigate *Consti-*

tution, built in 1797 and famous in the annals of the War of 1812.

Thomas Birch

Though Thomas Birch was born in England, his active life as an artist was spent entirely in the United States, whither he was brought by his father, William Birch the miniaturist in enamel, when but seven years old. He is the first of our marine painters; his earliest works celebrate the triumphs of American ships upon the high seas and were painted during the War of 1812. The more important of these large canvases, which measure about two and a half by four feet, picture "The Engagement of the *Constitution* and the *Guerrière*," "The Engagement of the *Wasp* and the *Frolic*," and "The Action of the Frigate *United States* and the *Macedonian*." His "Escape of the *Constitution*," a smaller canvas, may be seen at the New York Historical Society.

A number of Birch's fellow-countrymen had already pictured the Revolutionary naval engagement of September, 1779, off Flamborough Head on the

English coast, between John Paul Jones on the *Bonhomme Richard* and Captain Pearson on the *Serapis*. The best of these canvases is that by Richard Paton, painted the year of the engagement, exhibited at the Royal Academy in 1780, engraved that year, and now privately owned in this country. The scene at sundown or early twilight is admirably composed, and the painting has much the quality of a similiar subject from the brush of one of the better of the seventeenth-century Dutch masters.

Samuel F. B. Morse

The early reputation of Samuel F. B. Morse in England rests upon the historical picture from the classics entitled "The Dying Hercules," painted while the artist was working as a pupil in the studio of Benjamin West, in 1812, and exhibited at the Royal Academy the following year. The success of this canvas of heroic size led to his undertaking a similar work, "The Judgment of Jupiter in the Case of Apollo, Marpessa and Idas." The latter picture was quite as successful at the Royal Academy of 1815, but upon Morse's return to the United States, was shown for sale in his studio in Boston for more than a year without eliciting a single inquiry respecting the price.

After an interval of several years, in which Morse accumulated a modest fortune painting cabinet portraits in Charleston, South Carolina, he removed to Washington, D. C., in order to paint a large view of the interior of the House of Representatives, with portraits of the members. This huge canvas, eight by nine feet in size, was exhibited at a loss of hundreds of dollars and effectually discouraged further efforts at historic composition on Morse's part.

Asher B. Durand

Already noted in these pages as a portrait- and landscape-painter, Asher B. Durand painted at least two historical subjects. The first, dating from 1833, pictures "The Capture of Major André," and the other, a small canvas, represents "The Last Interview between Washington and Harvey Birch."

Robert F. Weir

Born in New Rochelle, New York, Robert W. Weir (the father of John F. and Julian Alden

Weir, both well-known painters of a later day), eventually became a pupil of John Wesley Jarvis. In 1832 he was made a member of the National Academy. As professor of drawing at the West Point Military Academy, he taught for over forty years.

Weir's large picture "The Embarkation of the Pilgrims" is in the rotunda of the Capitol at Washington. Besides that work he painted "The Landing of Henry Hudson" and "The Last Communion of Henry Clay." His portrait of General Winfield Scott may be seen at the Metropolitan Museum of Art in New York City.

J. B. Stearnes

J. B. Stearnes, born in Vermont in 1810, studied at the National Academy in New York City, of which he became a member in 1848. Though he practised portraiture almost exclusively, he nevertheless painted several large historical compositions, one of which, "The British in Council with the Indians," was engraved by T. Doney.

William Page

William Page was a pupil of Samuel F. B. Morse and of the National Academy, from which institution he received a premium for drawing in 1827. He practised as a portrait-painter in Albany, New York, in 1828 and 1829, and later had a studio in Boston. Among his historical canvases were "The Infancy of Henry IV" and "Farragut in the Shrouds of the *Hartford*," depicting the entry of the ship into Mobile Bay.

William Ranney

William Ranney was born in Middletown, Connecticut. His early manhood was spent in the United States Army, in which, during the Texan War, he became familiar with the life of the hunter and the Indian. He later settled in West Hoboken, New Jersey, where he painted a number of canvases suggested by his experiences as a soldier. They include "Boone and His Companions Discovering Kentucky," "The Burial of De Soto," and "The Sale of Manhattan by the Indians."

Yale Art Gallery, New Haven, Connecticut

PLATE LX

THE DEATH OF MONTGOMFRY, QUEBEC

Painted in 1786 by John Trumbull

Tompkins H. Matteson

Tompkins H. Matteson was born in the little village of Peterboro, Madison County, New York, in 1813, and named by his father, who was a sagacious politician, for Governor Tompkins of New York. He studied art first with an itinerant silhouette-painter. While still a mere youth he left home on foot, with a knapsack and a box of crayons, making portraits for a few shillings each and journeying as far as Albany.

Later, John Trumbull advised him and encouraged his efforts, and finally, in 1839, he opened a studio in New York City, where for several years he practised successfully as a portrait-painter. His historical pictures, which apparently were executed in the intervals between sittings for portraits, include "The Spirit of '76," "Captain Glen Claiming the Prisoners after the Burning of Schenectady," "Lafayette at Olmutz," "Washington's Inaugural," and "Elliott Preaching to the Indians."

Edwin White

A native of Massachusetts, born in South Hadley, Edwin White studied in Paris and Düsseldorf. Returning to this country, he established himself in New York City, where he was elected to the National Academy in 1849. While a student abroad he painted the first of a number of notable historical canvases, "The Requiem of De Soto." This he followed with the "Separation of the Pilgrims at Delft Haven," "Columbus partaking of the Sacrament on the Morning of His Embarkation," "The Signing of the Compact on Board the Mayflower," and "Pocahontas Informing Smith of the Conspiracy."

White's best-known work, however, is his "Washington Resigning His Commission at Annapolis," painted for the Senate Chamber of the State of Maryland. He continued to picture historical events long after 1850, including in his later works several Civil War subjects.

Charles Deas

Charles Deas, a grandson of Ralph Izard, was born in Philadelphia, where he was inspired by visits to the Pennsylvania Academy and the studio of Thomas Sully to undertake an artistic career. He studied in the National Academy school in New York and his earliest works were genre pictures. He later visited a brother in the army, stationed at Fort Crawford in the far West, and painted a number of canvases depicting Indian subjects, like "The Wounded Pawnee," "Hunters on the Prairie," "A Group of Sioux," "The Indian Guide," and "The Voyageur."

Emanuel Leutze

Before he began to paint portraits, Emanuel Leutze, while a student at Düsseldorf in the early eighteen-forties, painted "Columbus before the Council of Salamanca," which was immediately purchased by the Art Union of that city. This was followed by "Columbus before the Queen" and later by "Columbus in Chains," which latter picture first brought him fame in this country. Henry T. Tuckerman, the best contemporary critic of art, said of it:

"The figure of Columbus is noble and impressive. The felicity with which so many forms are grouped, the emotion or its absence in the different faces, the fine harmony of coloring, and the variety of costume, make the picture . . . delightful and satisfactory."

George W. Flagg

The most important of George W. Flagg's historical canvases, "The Landing of the Pilgrims" and "Washington Receiving His Mother's Blessing," were painted in New Haven, Connecticut, where the artist was born and where he first practised painting professionally. At a much later date he pictured "The Landing of the Atlantic Cable."

Daniel Huntington

During the eighteen-forties, Daniel Huntington, in the intervals when he was not engaged in portrait-painting, which was his chief occupation at that period, executed several historical compositions, including "Henry the Eighth and Catharine Parr" and "Mary Signing Lady Jane Grey's Death-Warrant." Many years after, he painted a picture of "Mrs. Washington's Reception" during her residence in the Presidential mansion, in which he grouped sixty-four figures of national importance, each one a portrait from an original by John Singleton Copley, Gilbert Stuart, Edward Green Malbone or from family likenesses in the possession of living descendants, much in the manner made familiar by John Trumbull's earlier historical compositions.

PART VII

RELIGIOUS PAINTERS

LIST OF PAINTERS

Gustavus Hesselius	Swedish	1682–1755
Benjamin West	American	1728–1820
Washington Allston	American	1779–1843
William Jewett	American	1795–1874
Robert W. Weir	American	1803–1889
William S. Mount	American	1807–1868
William Page	American	1811–1885
William Rimmer	English	1816–1843
George W. Flagg	American	1816–1897
Daniel Huntington	American	1816–1906

PART VII

RELIGIOUS PAINTERS

GUSTAVUS HESSELIUS

THE large picture of "The Last Supper," approximately three feet high by ten feet wide, which the Swedish artist Gustavus Hesselius painted in 1722 for Saint Barnabas Church, Queen Anne's Parish, Maryland, was the first religious picture executed in America. It follows pretty closely in arrangement Italian models dating from the fifteenth century. Charles Henry Hart has pointed out the similarity of the composition to that of "The Last Supper" of Andrea del Sarto in Florence, with which Hesselius might have been acquainted through engravings—though he reverted to Andrea del Castagno's earlier representation in placing the figure of Judas as sitting apart, apparently in contemplation of the projected betrayal. The only early religious picture painted in this country, it is a work of considerable distinction, and should be seen to be appreciated.

Hesselius was a cousin of Swedenborg, probably was of a deeply religious nature, and unquestionably found in the portrayal of this scene peculiar satisfaction. Whatever it may lack in anatomical accuracy and dramatic effect, the artist has succeeded in imbuing it with a sense of moral exaltation which effectually precludes the possibility of dismissing it as a merely commonplace graphic performance more truly illustrative than artistic. Though the draftsmanship is primitive, here and there a well-modeled head or successfully drawn hand catches the eye, and, generally speaking, the figures are not badly articulated. One feels life in arms and legs, as well as in momentary posture and movement arrested beneath robes and mantles.

Gustavus Hesselius was primarily a portrait-painter, and it has been said that the gentleness of the apostle John's expression may be better understood if one accepts the theory that for this head the artist's wife, Lydia, was the model. The likeness of his wife at the Pennsylvania Historical Society in Philadelphia would seem to justify us in the belief that such was the case.

Yale Art Gallery, New Haven, Connecticut

PLATE LXI

THE BATTLE OF BUNKER HILL

By John Trumbull

Religious Painters

Benjamin West

In his capacity as painter to the King of England, Benjamin West produced in his London studio the most ambitious pictures of a religious character ever created by a native-born American artist. His series of twenty-eight subjects from the Old and New Testaments, for which he received over twenty-one thousand pounds, constitutes one of the greatest undertakings of any painter since the masters of the Italian Renaissance. In order rightly to appreciate West's achievement, one must remember that all of these canvases were of heroic proportions.

Of his other Biblical subjects, "The Descent of the Holy Ghost on Christ at Jordan," measures ten by fourteen feet, "The Crucifixion," sixteen by twenty-eight feet, and "The Ascension," twelve by eighteen feet. His ambitions may have exceeded his abilities, but they are no less an impressive indication of his ideals and the prodigious labor he performed in his efforts to realize them. Nor should we forget that in his day those great canvases made a profound impression upon all spectators.

Washington Allston

The religious pictures of Washington Allston, though not of such generous proportions as Benjamin West's, are more carefully planned as compositions and therefore considerably more effective. In such a canvas as "The Dead Man Revived by Touching the Bones of the Prophet Elijah," in the Philadelphia Academy of Art, one encounters a two-sectional picture in which the main figure occupies the foreground, which is linked to the upper composition by the large figure at the right, looking down upon the man rising from the dead. This is a much better work than Allston's "Jeremiah Dictating His Prophecy," at the Yale Art Gallery, but the large, unfinished "Belshazzar's Feast" at the Boston Museum, even in its imperfect state, exhibits the artist's mastery of impressive design.

Besides these canvases, Allston painted "The Angel Releasing St. Peter," "Christ Healing," "Elijah in the Desert," "Jacob's Dream," and others. His idea that in a large composition the principal figure should be unmistakable resulted in his enlarging it unnecessarily at times—to such an extent as to defeat the balance of masses which is so vital an element of impressive design. This is exemplified in his "Jeremiah Dictating His Prophecy."

William Jewett

For over forty years widely known as the partner of Samuel L. Waldo in the most successful of all native American coöperative portrait-painting associations, William Jewett, while still a pupil in Waldo's studio in New York City, exhibited at the American Academy in that city several Biblical subjects. Their present location is unknown.

Robert W. Weir

The first of Robert W. Weir's religious pictures, "Christ and Nicodemus," and "The Angel Releasing Saint Peter," were painted abroad, while the artist was working in Florence. They were inspired by the paintings he saw in Italy, where the greatest works of art are associated with the Church. Weir was of a deeply religious nature and the little church of the "Holy Innocents" at West Point, where he was professor of drawing for so many years, is a memorial to his devotion, having been erected chiefly through his efforts.

William S. Mount

William Sidney Mount, born on Long Island, studied at the National Academy school and later, for over forty years, had a studio in New York City. In 1828, at the very beginning of his career, he painted a picture of "The Raising of the Daughter of Jairus," the single religious subject from his hand recorded. He is known best as a portrait-painter and for his folk pictures, such as "Raffling for the Goose," now at the Metropolitan Museum of Art in New York City.

William Page

A student of Samuel F. B. Morse, and preëminently a portrait-painter, William Page painted a number of Biblical canvases, including "Ruth and Naomi," now at the New York Historical Society, a "Holy Family," in the Boston Museum, and a "Head of Christ."

William Rimmer

Descended from one of the royal families of France, William Rimmer was born and reared in England, where his father had settled. He came to the United States in 1818, and about 1838 painted a picture representing Adam and Eve mourning over the body of Abel. He was a very gifted artist and, besides compositions of this character, painted portraits and worked in sculpture.

Incidentally Rimmer was a practising physician, and in his professional capacity as well as in his rôle as a sculptor he acquired an accurate knowledge of anatomy which is evident in the figures in his canvases. In the eighteen-forties he pictured "The Infant Saviour," and a large altarpiece with life-size representations of the Virgin, the Child, and Joseph. His other religious works inelude a "Crucifixion," and an "Infant St. Peter."

George W. Flagg

It is not surprising that a number of the works of George W. Flagg are religious in character, for this artist was a nephew of Washington Allston, the preeminent exponent of religious painting in America in his day. It is natural that his nephew, working in Boston where Allston had his studio, should try his hand at it also. Allston, seeing one of Flagg's earlier attempts—"Jacob and Rachel at the Well"—said to him, "Now you may consider yourself an artist." Flagg later painted a picture of "The Good Samaritan."

Daniel Huntington

The religious compositions of Daniel Huntington were in their day very highly esteemed and undoubtedly did much to establish his reputation as an artist of great ability, though he later turned his attention almost exclusively to portrait-painting. The "Early Christian Prisoners," "Christiana and her Children Escaping from the Valley of the Shadow of Death," "The Women of Samaria at the Well," "The Communion of the Sick," and the "Mercy's Dream," now at the Metropolitan Museum of Art in New York City, were the most famous of his religious pictures.

Religious Painters

This type of painting, at the time so highly regarded, is quite out of fashion to-day, and the present whereabouts of most of the above-named works is unknown.

PART VIII

GENRE PAINTERS

LIST OF PAINTERS

Henry Inman	American	1801–1846
John W. Edmonds	American	1806 ——
William S. Mount	American	1807–1868
George C. Lambdin	American	1807–1889
William Page	American	1811–1885
William S. Ranney	American	1813–1857
Tompkins H. Matteson	American	1813–1884
Louis Lang	German	1814?1893
James H. Beard	American	1815?——
Daniel Huntington	American	1816–1906
Frederick Fink	American	1817–1849
Edwin White	American	1817–1877
Richard M. Staigg	English	1817–1881
Thomas LeClear	American	1818–1882
Richard Caton Woodville	American	1820–1855

PART VIII

GENRE PAINTERS

THE picturing of scenes from everyday life did not really begin in America until the early years of the last century, and our artists generally confined themselves to rather literal representations, unrelieved by anything comparable to the humor of Thomas Rowlandson or the satire of William Hogarth, the great English genre painters.

HENRY INMAN

In the intervals of portrait- and miniature-painting, Henry Inman, as a young man, produced a number of genre pictures, among them the "Trout Fishing," and the "Mumble-the-Peg," recording in color his observations of contemporary life. Henry T. Tuckerman said of Inman that he was one of the most versatile of American artists and that he excelled as a painter of these cabinet pictures.

John W. Edmonds

The earliest native artist who was in reality a genre painter, John W. Edmonds, the son of General Samuel Edmonds, a Revolutionary officer, was born in Hudson, New York, in 1806. He was employed as a bank clerk in his native town until 1830, when he became cashier of the Hudson River Bank. Later he was cashier of the New York Leather Manufacturers' Bank and the old Mechanics' Bank on Wall Street, in New York City.

Edmonds's painting must have been indulged in rather as a recreation from the prosaic duties of banking. His subjects were of the homely, homey sort, with a certain realism about them that recommended them to the average taste of the time. When he was proposed as an associate of the National Academy the question of his eligibility as an artist was decided by the fact of his having sold pictures and being, therefore, a professional artist, though as indicated above he was a banker rather than a painter.

"Stealing Milk," "Bargaining," "Taking the Census," "The Beggar's Petition," and "Sparking"

Property of the Hon. Breckenridge Long, Washington, D. C.

PLATE LXII

THE CAPTURE OF MAJOR ANDRÉ

By John Trumbull

are among the titles of his many works. His "Sparking" was engraved by the Art Union.

William S. Mount

To-day probably the best known of our early painters of genre is William Sidney Mount, whose "Raffling for the Goose," painted in 1837, may be seen at the Metropolitan Museum of Art in New York City. His first picture of the type to win the attention of the public, however, was one called "Husking Corn." He also painted the "Farmers Nooning," the "Boys Gambling in a Barn," the "Turning the Grindstone," the "Bargaining for a Horse," and innumerable similar subjects, which found a ready sale at very respectable figures to collectors of his day.

George C. Lambdin

The son of James R. Lambdin the portrait-painter, George C. Lambdin, was born in Pittsburgh, Pennsylvania, in 1807. He studied art in Philadelphia with Edward Miles and Thomas Sully. His best pictures are those which represent poverty and illness, for he had a remarkable skill in the expression of pathos. One of his subjects, which was sent to Paris for exhibition and received favorable notice there, was entitled "The Last Sleep." Sentiment of a serious kind informs all his works with real interest as commentaries on life.

William Page

Though primarily a portrait-painter, William Page painted several genre pictures, probably as a diversion from his more serious efforts. One of them called "The Wife's Last Visit to her Condemned Husband" must have waited long for a purchaser. Another called the "Young Merchants," less harrowing, probably sold readily enough.

William S. Ranney

Better known as a painter of historical pictures, William S. Ranney has to his credit one recorded genre picture whose title, "The Old Oaken Bucket," leads one to think that it may be the earliest representation of the subject in American graphic art.

Tompkins H. Matteson

At the beginning of his career this artist, who has already been noticed as a portrait-painter, produced several genre pictures such as "Whirling the Platter," which was perhaps a game, now obsolete, and "Redeeming Forfeits."

Louis Lang

The son of a German portrait-painter, Louis Lang, born in Waldser, Würtemberg, came to the United States in 1838 and settled in Philadelphia. A representative example of his genre painting is the picture called "The Sewing Society."

James H. Beard

The eldest son of Captain James Beard and grandson of Judge James Beard of New Haven, Connecticut, James H. Beard the artist was born in Buffalo, New York, but in his infancy his parents moved to Ohio, where they finally settled in Painesville. His first master in art was an unrecorded itinerent painter named Hanks.

James Beard's first works to attract attention were "The Long Bill," "The Land Speculator," and "The North Carolina Emigrants." He later painted portraits of John Quincy Adams and General William Henry Harrison.

Daniel Huntington

Besides Daniel Huntington's numerous historical compositions and portraits, two genre paintings from his hand are recorded by Henry T. Tuckerman, "The Counterfeit Note," and "A Bar-room Politician." He also painted other similar works, including the "Old Lawyer," and "A Toper Asleep."

Frederick Fink

A grandson of Major Fink of Revolutionary fame, Frederick Fink was born at Little Falls, New York, December 18, 1817, and started out as a student of medicine with a doctor in Albany. He later joined his brother in business, but finally went to New York City and studied art with Samuel F. B. Morse. In the course of his short professional career—he died at the age of thirty-three years—he made an enviable reputation as a genre painter. His subjects included "A Negro Wood-sawyer," "The Young Thieves," and "The Shipwrecked Mariner."

Edwin White

One of the first of Edwin White's works to receive favorable attention was a genre picture en-

Property of Mrs. R. N. Warrington

PLATE LXIII

THE LAST SUPPER

Painted 1721–22 by Gustavus Hesselius

titled "Age's Reverie," now at the West Point Military Academy. Though most of his subsequent productions were in the field of historical and religious art, he continued to paint occasional genre subjects such as "The Antiquary," "The Olden Time," "Tired of Work," "Hop Scotch," "Sunday Morning," and others of similar interest.

Richard M. Staigg

Born September 7, 1817, in Leeds, England, Richard M. Staigg worked there for a time in an architect's office. In 1831 he came to the United States and settled in Newport, Rhode Island, where he was encouraged by Washington Allston. He studied there with Jane Stuart and began his professional career as a portrait-miniaturist. Several of his early ivories were taken to England by friends and exhibited at the Royal Academy. Of his later genre pictures, his "Cat's Cradle," shown at the National Academy, was highly praised by contemporary critics. Other of his works in this field were "The Little Crossing-Sweeper," "The Little Gate-Keeper," "Knitting," "Skaters," and "Somebody's Coming."

Thomas LeClear

This artist, born in Owego, New York, March 11, 1818, when but nine years old attempted a portrait, using lamp-black, Venetian red, and white lead, on a piece of pine board. As may be readily imagined, he was encouraged in his artistic efforts and he later became successful as a professional portrait-painter. His likeness of William Page the artist may now be seen at the Corcoran Art Gallery in Washington, D. C. During the eighteen-forties he painted a number of genre pictures, among them the "Marble Players," the "Young America," and "The Reprimand."

Richard Caton Woodville

The last of our genre painters included here, Richard Caton Woodville, born in Baltimore, Maryland, was the most prolific of the early American practitioners of genre painting. He went abroad for study and worked in the schools of Düsseldorf. His first recognition in the United States as an artist came through the exhibition of a picture of humble pretensions, showing the interior of a bar-room.

In 1847, Woodville was represented at the Art-Union in New York City by a picture called "The Card Players," which was engraved, and in 1848 by "The Cavalier's Return," and "Mexican News." His fame was established prior to 1850 by a small work of exquisite finish entitled "A Man Holding a Book." His "Game of Chess" was painted in 1850.

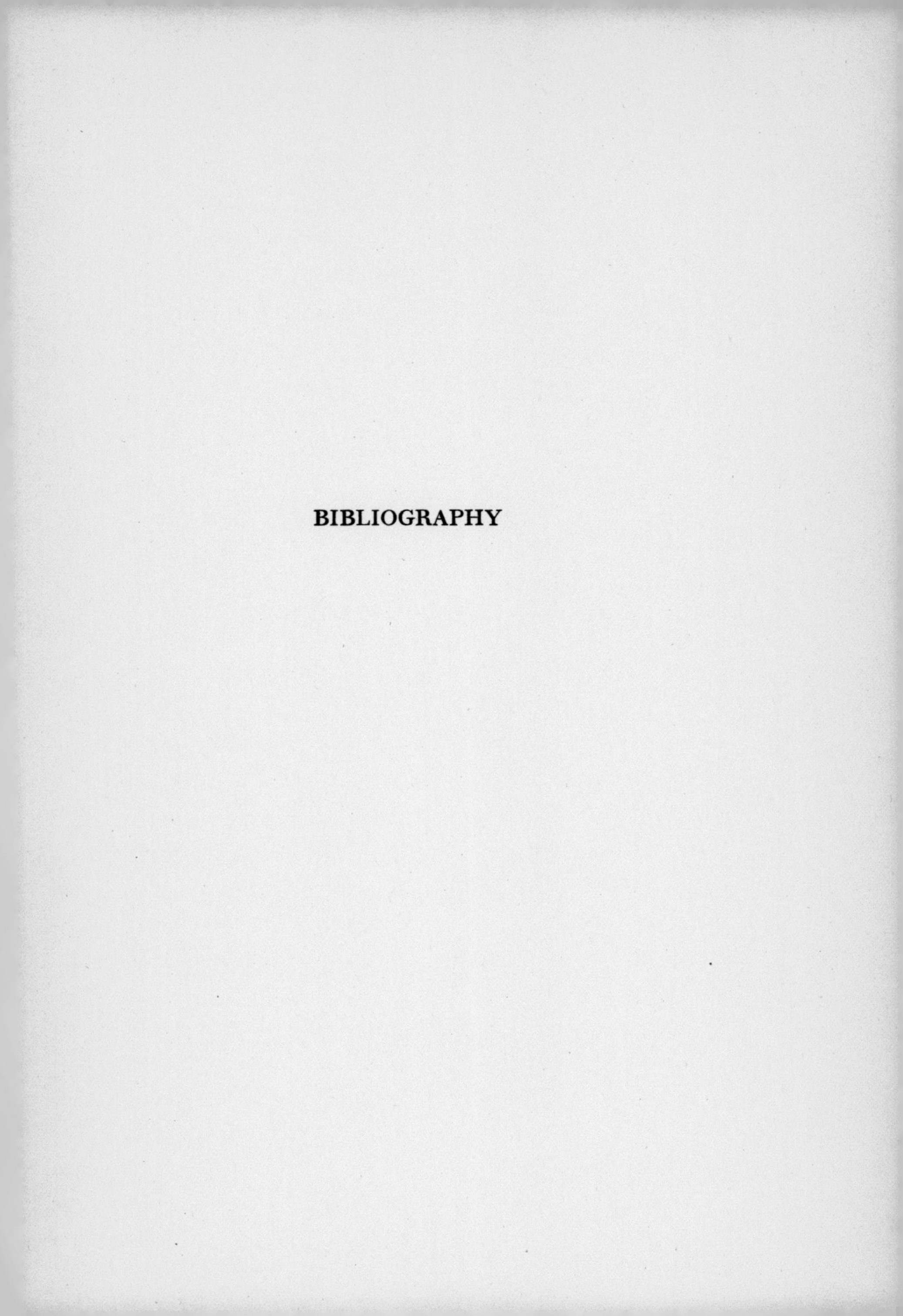

BIBLIOGRAPHY

BIBLIOGRAPHY

Amory, Martha Babcock. *The Domestic and Artistic Life of John Singleton Copley.* Houghton Mifflin Company, Boston, 1882.

Anonymous. *Catalogue of the Loan Exhibition of 100 Colonial Portraits at the Museum of Fine Arts,* Boston, 1930.

Audubon, Mrs. John J. (Editor). *The Life of John James Audubon.* G. P. Putnam's Sons, New York, 1883.

Bartlett, Truman H. *The Art Life of William Rimmer.* J. R. Osgood & Co., Boston, 1882.

Bayley, Frank W. *The Life and Works of John Singleton Copley.* The Taylor Press, Boston, 1915.

Clarke, Thomas B. *Portraits by Early American Artists of the Seventeenth, Eighteenth, and Nineteenth Centuries. Collected by Thomas B. Clarke.* Philadelphia Museum of Art. Philadelphia, 1928.

Coburn, Frederick W. *John Smibert.* "Art in America," Vol. XVII, No. 4 (June, 1929), p. 175.

Jeremiah Dummer's Portraits of John Coney, Silversmith, and Mary Atwater Coney, His Wife. "Art in America," Vol. XVIII, No. 5 (August, 1930), p. 244.

Mather Brown. "Art in America," Vol. XI, No. 5 (August, 1923), p. 252.

Cunningham, Henry Winchester. *Christian Remick: An Early Boston Artist.* The Club of Odd Volumes, Boston, 1904.

Dunlap, William. *History of the Arts of Design in the United States.* The Bayley-Goodspeed edition of 1918, 3 vols., Boston.

Bibliography

Durand, John. *The Life and Times of A. B. Durand.* Charles Scribner's Sons, New York, 1894.

Fielding, Mantle. *Dictionary of American Painters, Sculptors, and Engravers.* Fielding, Philadelphia, no date.

Gilbert Stuart's Portraits of Washington. Fielding, Philadelphia, 1923.

Flagg, Jared B. *The Life and Letters of Washington Allston.* Charles Scribner's Sons, New York, 1892.

Foote, Henry Wilder. *Robert Feke: Colonial Portrait Painter.* Harvard University Press, Cambridge, Mass., 1930.

French, H. W. *Art and Artists in Connecticut.* Boston, 1879.

Galt, John. *The Life, Studies and Works of Benjamin West.* T. Cadett & W. Davies, London, 1820.

Halsey, R. T. H. *Malbone and His Miniatures.* "Scribner's Magazine," Vol. XLVII, No. 5 (May, 1910), p. 558.

Hart, Charles Henry. *Portrait of Jean Antoine Houdon Painted by Rembrandt Peale.* "Art in America," Vol. III, No. 2 (February, 1915), p. 78.

Portrait of Jacques Louis David Painted by Rembrandt Peale. "Art in America," Vol. III, No. 5 (August, 1915), p. 257.

Portrait of John Grimes Painted by Matthew Harris Jouett. "Art in America," Vol. IV, No. 3 (April, 1916), p. 175.

Portrait of James Ward, R. A., Painted by Gilbert Stuart. "Art in America," Vol. IV, No. 2 (February, 1916), p. 114.

Portrait of Richard Mentor Johnson Painted by John Neagle. "Art in America," Vol. IV, No. 5 (August, 1916), p. 288.

Portrait of James Ross Painted by Thomas Sully. "Art in America," Vol. IV, No. 6 (September, 1916), p. 340.

The Gordon Family Painted by Henry Benbridge. "Art in America," Vol. VI, No. 4 (June, 1918), p. 191.

Bibliography

Huger Smith, Alice R. and D. E. *Charles Fraser*. Sherman, New York, 1924.

Knox, Katharine McCook. *The Sharples*. Yale University Press, New Haven, 1930.

Lester, C. Edwards. *Artists of America*. Baker & Scribner, New York, 1846.

Marceau, Henri. *The Last Supper by Gustavus Hesselius*. "Pennsylvania Museum Bulletin," Vol. XXVI, No. 142 (May, 1931), p. 11.

Morgan, John Hill. *Early American Painters Illustrated by Examples in the Collection of the New York Historical Society*. New York, 1921.

Paintings by John Trumbull at Yale University. Yale University Press, New Haven, Conn., 1926.

A Sketch of John Ramage, Miniature Painter. The New York Historical Society, New York, 1930.

Noble, Louis L. *The Course of Empire, Voyage of Life, and Other Pictures of Thomas Cole, N. A.*, with selections from his letters and miscellaneous writings. New York, 1853.

Perkins, Augustus T. *Sketch of the Life of John Singleton Copley*. J. R. Osgood & Co., Boston, 1873.

Piers, Harry. *Robert Field: Portrait Painter in Oils, Miniatures, and Water-Colors, and Engraver*. Sherman, New York, 1927.

Price, Gen. Samuel W. *The Old Masters of the Bluegrass*. Filson Club Publications, No. 17. Louisville, Kentucky, 1902.

Sherman, Frederic Fairchild. *Early American Portraiture*. Sherman, New York, 1930.

John Ramage: A Biographical Sketch and a List of His Portrait Miniatures. Sherman, New York, 1929.

Bibliography

Sweetser, M. F. *Allston*, in the series of "Artist Biographies." Boston, 1879.

Tolman, Ruel P. *Newly Discovered Miniatures by Edward Greene Malbone.* "Antiques," Vol. XVI, No. 5 (November, 1929), p. 377.

Trumbull, John. *Autobiography, Reminiscences and Letters from 1756 to 1841.* W. L. Hamlen, New Haven, Conn., 1841.

Tuckerman, Henry T. *American Artist Life.* G. P. Putnam's Sons, New York, 1867.

Wehle, Harry B. *American Miniatures, 1730–1850.* Metropolitan Museum of Art, New York, 1927.

Wharton, Anne Hollingsworth. *Heirlooms in Miniatures.* J. B. Lippincott Company, Philadelphia, 1898.

INDEX

Index

Index

Index

Index